MW01630818

PRAYER JOURNAL FOR TEEN BOYS

Create Meaningful Connections with God, Discover Your True Purpose, and Strengthen Your Confidence Through Daily Prayer Practices

Infinite Echo Publishing

TABLE OF CONTENTS

Introduction 4

- Welcome to Your Prayer Journey
- How to Use This Journal
- Why Prayer Matters in Today's World

Chapter 1: Building a Daily Connection with God 9
Chapter 2: Strengthening Your Identity in Christ 22
Chapter 3: Overcoming Challenges Through Faith 35
Chapter 4: Building Strong Relationships 48
Chapter 5: Finding Peace in a Busy World 61
Chapter 6: Developing Godly Wisdom 74
Chapter 7: Living Out Your Faith 87
Chapter 8: Growing Spiritually Through Challenges 100
Chapter 9: Dreaming Big with God 113
Chapter 10: Gratitude and Contentment 126
Chapter 11: Reflecting on Your Journey 139
Chapter 12: Becoming a Leader in Faith 152
Chapter 13: Preparing for the Next Chapter 165

Final Reflections 179

- Reflecting on Your Year in Prayer
- Spiritual Goals for the Year Ahead
- Keys to Continuing Your Faith Journey

INTRODUCTION

Welcome to your Prayer Journal!

Life as a teenager is a wild and exhilarating adventure. It's a time of discovery, growth, and excitement, but it's also a time of uncertainty, challenges, and questions. You're stepping into a world full of possibilities—navigating friendships, sports, school, family expectations, and figuring out who you really are. It's a lot to juggle, and sometimes it can feel like there's more pressure than peace, more chaos than clarity.

But what if I told you there's a way to find strength and calm in the middle of it all? A way to stay grounded and focused while the world around you feels unpredictable? The truth is, you don't have to figure everything out on your own. You have a powerful source of guidance, wisdom, and strength—your relationship with God.

This isn't about rules or rituals. It's about something much bigger: building a real connection with the Creator who knows you better than anyone else. It's about having a space where you can unload your worries, celebrate your victories, and find direction when life feels like it's spinning too fast.

Think of this journal as your personal retreat—a safe place where you can hit pause, catch your breath, and tune out the noise of the world. Here, you'll discover how prayer can be more than just words—it can be a conversation with God that shapes your life in incredible ways. You'll find tools to reflect on your day, ask for help when you need it, and grow into the strong, confident, and kind person you are.

Each week in this journal is designed to help you take one step closer to God. You'll explore themes like courage, patience, kindness, and purpose while learning to handle challenges like peer pressure, stress, and doubts with faith and confidence. You'll reflect on what really matters, celebrate the gifts and talents God has given you, and dream big about your future.

This isn't just about surviving the teenage years—it's about thriving. It's about discovering how God's love and wisdom can transform every part of your life. It's about becoming a young man who isn't just strong but grounded; who isn't just brave but faithful; who isn't just successful but guided by purpose.

So grab your pen, open your heart, and let's get started on this journey together. You don't have to be perfect, and you don't need all the answers. You just need to show up, be honest, and let God meet you where you are. Because with Him, every twist, turn, and challenge in life becomes part of a bigger and more beautiful story—your story.

Welcome to the adventure. Let's make it count.

How to Use This Journal

This journal is more than just a book—it's your personal guide to building a stronger relationship with God over the next 52 weeks. Think of it as a companion, a coach, and a safe space all rolled into one.

Here's how you can get the most out of it:

Start with an Open Heart
Set aside time each week, even just a few minutes, to sit down with this journal. Be honest with yourself and with God. There's no "right" or "wrong" way to approach this—just come as you are.

Weekly Themes
Each week has a specific focus, such as courage, forgiveness, gratitude, or trusting God. Start by reading the weekly devotion, which introduces the theme and includes a Scripture verse to reflect on.

Reflect and Write
After reading, you'll find guided prompts to help you dive deeper. These questions are designed to make you think, reflect, and connect with God. Don't rush—take your time to answer honestly.

Daily Connection
Each week also includes space for daily prayers. Use this section to jot down your thoughts, prayers, and anything else on your heart. It doesn't have to be perfect—just let it flow.

Look Back and Celebrate
As you go through the year, take moments to flip back through the pages. You'll be amazed at how much you've grown spiritually and personally. Celebrate the victories and learn from the challenges.

This journal is yours, so make it personal. Scribble, underline, draw, or highlight anything that stands out to you. The more you pour into it, the more you'll get out of it.

Why Prayer Matters in Today's World

The world you're growing up in is fast-paced, noisy, and sometimes overwhelming. You're constantly bombarded with expectations, decisions, and distractions. Social media, school pressures, friendships, and personal challenges can make it hard to feel centered or even hopeful.

This is why prayer is more important than ever. Prayer isn't just a spiritual activity—it's your lifeline. It's a way to pause, reset, and reconnect with God in the middle of the chaos.

When you pray, you're not just talking to a distant being—you're speaking to the One who created you, loves you, and knows exactly what you're going through. Prayer reminds you that you're never alone, no matter how hard life gets.
Prayer also gives you perspective. It helps you zoom out from the immediate problems and see the bigger picture. When you bring your worries to God, you're reminded that He's in control, even when things feel out of control.

But prayer isn't just about asking for things. It's about listening, too. It's about letting God's wisdom guide you in making decisions, His peace calm your fears, and His strength carry you through challenges.

In today's world, where it's easy to feel lost or disconnected, prayer anchors you. It's like having a compass that always points you in the right direction, no matter how uncertain the path ahead may seem.

Through this journal, you'll discover how prayer can be a powerful tool to navigate life's ups and downs. It's not just about solving problems—it's about building a relationship with God that brings purpose, confidence, and joy into every part of your life.

Let's take this journey together and see just how powerful prayer can be.

CHAPTER 1

BUILDING A DAILY CONNECTION WITH GOD

A strong relationship with God begins with consistent daily habits. This chapter focuses on discovering the importance of prayer, gratitude, and Scripture as tools to deepen your connection with Him. You'll learn that spending time with God doesn't have to be complicated—it's about creating moments in your day to share your heart, seek His guidance, and grow in faith. These practices will lay the foundation for a relationship that carries you through life's ups and downs.

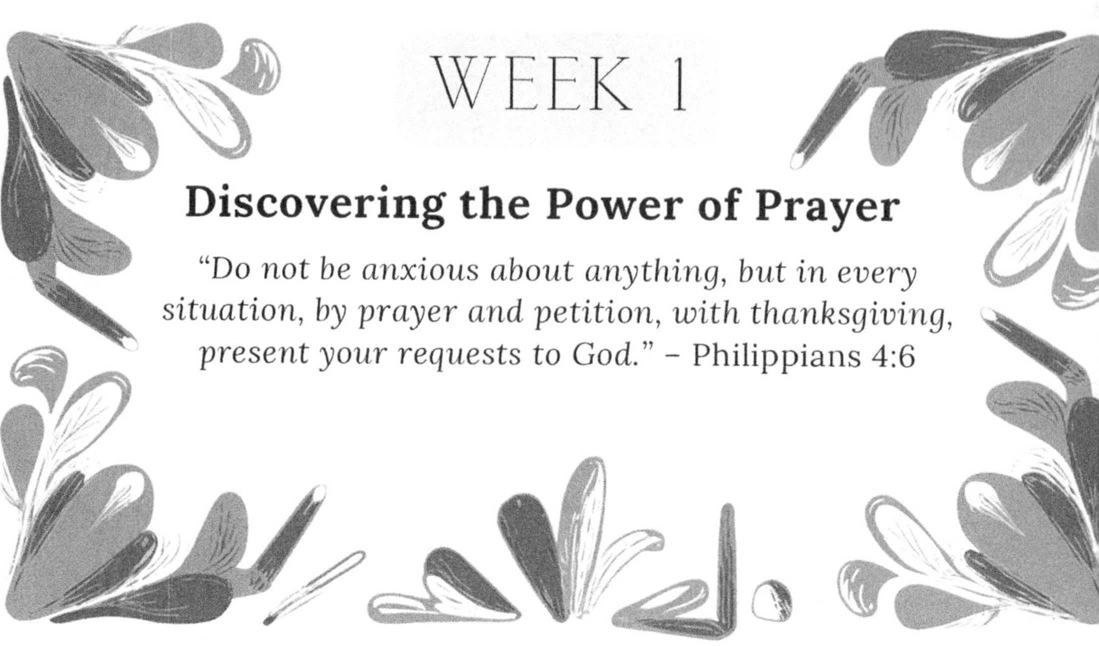

WEEK 1

Discovering the Power of Prayer

"Do not be anxious about anything, but in every situation, by prayer and petition, with thanksgiving, present your requests to God." – Philippians 4:6

REFLECTION

Prayer is a powerful tool that connects us directly to God. It's not about having the perfect words or saying the right things—it's about opening your heart to Him. When you pray, you're inviting God into your life, your struggles, and your victories. This verse reminds us that we don't have to carry our worries alone. Through prayer, we can hand over our fears, anxieties, and concerns to God, trusting that He is in control. Prayer isn't just about asking for help; it's also about thanking God for His blessings and trusting Him to guide you.

WEEKLY CHALLENGE

Set aside five minutes each day this week to pray. Start with something simple: thank God for one thing in your life, ask for His help with one challenge, and share one thing you're excited or nervous about. Write down how you feel after each prayer in your journal.

Share your thoughts:

JOURNAL QUESTIONS

What do you think makes prayer powerful?

How do you feel after you spend time praying?

What is one specific thing you want to ask God for this week?

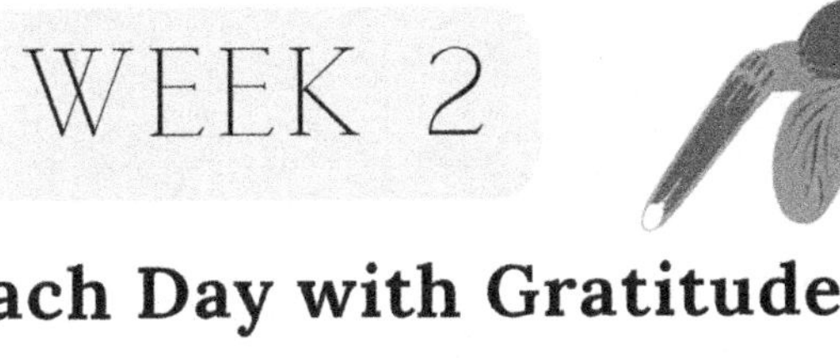

WEEK 2

Starting Each Day with Gratitude

"Give thanks in all circumstances; for this is God's will for you in Christ Jesus." – 1 Thessalonians 5:18

REFLECTION

It's easy to get caught up in the negatives—what's going wrong, what you don't have, or what you wish were different. But this verse reminds us that gratitude is a choice, and it's a powerful one. When you start your day by giving thanks, you set the tone for the hours ahead. Gratitude shifts your focus from what's missing to what you already have, and it opens your heart to see God's blessings, even in tough situations. Gratitude also deepens your relationship with God by acknowledging His presence and provision in your life.

WEEKLY CHALLENGE

Each morning this week, write down three things you're thankful for before you start your day. They can be big or small—anything from a good night's sleep to a kind word from a friend. At the end of the week, reflect on how practicing gratitude has affected your attitude and outlook.

Share your thoughts:

PRAYER TIPS

1 Begin your morning by thanking God for three things in your life.

2 Use your journal to write a gratitude prayer each day.

3 When something goes wrong, pause and think of one thing you can still be grateful for.

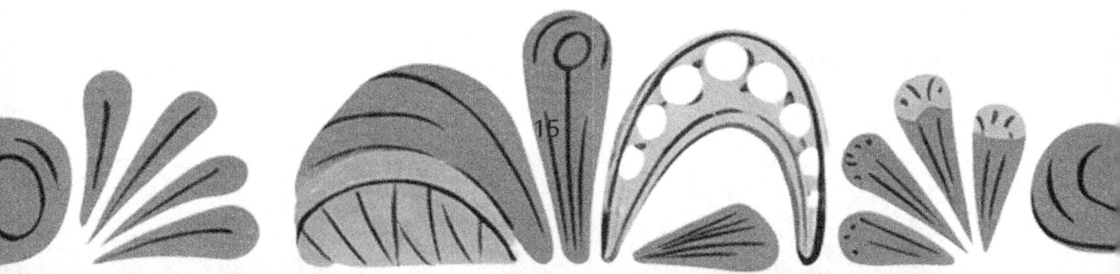

WEEK 3

Understanding God's Word

"Your word is a lamp to my feet and a light to my path."
– Psalm 119:105

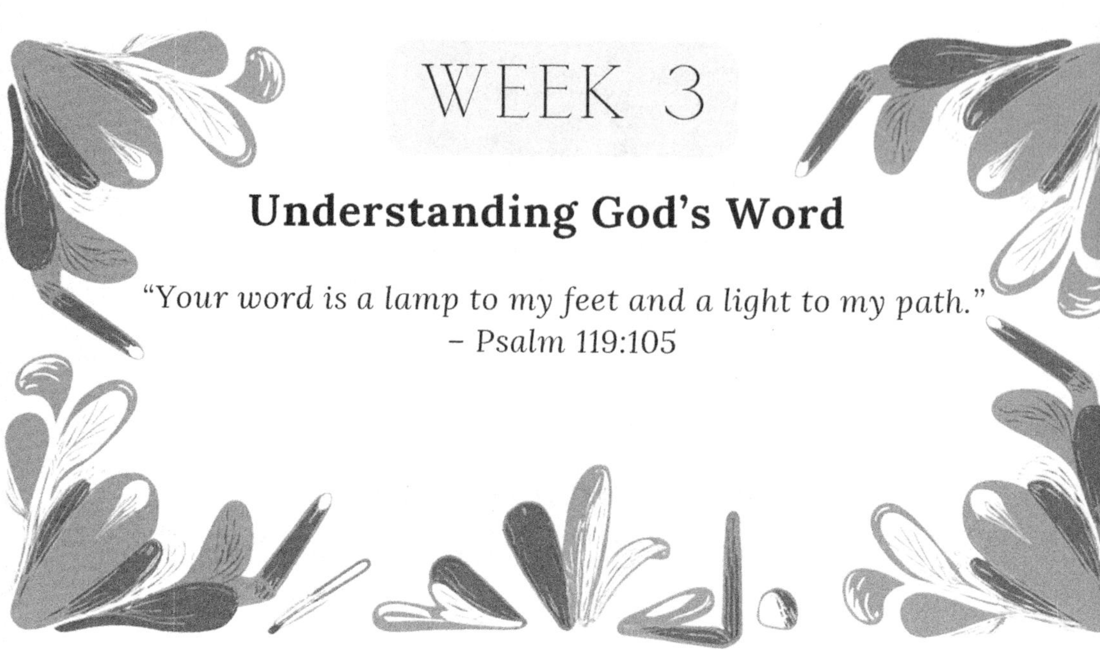

REFLECTION

The Bible is more than just a book; it's God's way of speaking to us. This verse describes how Scripture serves as a guide, offering wisdom, clarity, and direction when life feels confusing or overwhelming. By spending time reading and reflecting on God's Word, you allow His truth to shape your thoughts, decisions, and actions. Understanding the Bible doesn't happen overnight—it's a journey of learning and discovery. Each time you open its pages, you're taking another step toward understanding God's plan for your life.

WEEKLY CHALLENGE

Choose one Bible verse to read and reflect on each day this week. Write down what it means to you and how it applies to your life. Use your journal to jot down any questions or insights, and pray for God to help you understand His Word more deeply.

Share your thoughts:

JOURNAL QUESTIONS

What is one Bible verse that stands out to you this week? Why?

How can you make reading the Bible a regular part of your life?

How does God's Word guide you when you face tough choices?

WEEK 4

Developing a Habit of Daily Devotion

"But seek first His kingdom and His righteousness, and all these things will be given to you as well." – Matthew 6:33

REFLECTION

In a busy world, it's easy to let your faith take a back seat to other priorities. This verse encourages us to put God first—to make seeking Him a daily habit. When you prioritize time with God, you'll notice a difference in how you approach your day and handle challenges. A daily devotion doesn't have to be long or complicated; it's simply about setting aside time to focus on God through prayer, reading Scripture, and reflection. Developing this habit strengthens your relationship with Him and helps you stay grounded, no matter what's happening around you.

WEEKLY CHALLENGE

Pick a consistent time each day—morning, afternoon, or evening—and dedicate it to spending time with God. Use this journal to guide you: read the week's Bible verse, reflect on its meaning, and write a short prayer. By the end of the week, see how this habit has impacted your relationship with God and your overall mindset.

Share your thoughts:

PRAYER TIPS

1 Set a consistent time each day for prayer or devotion—even if it's just five minutes.

2 Find a quiet spot where you won't be distracted.

3 Use a devotional app or bookmark your favorite Bible passage to start.

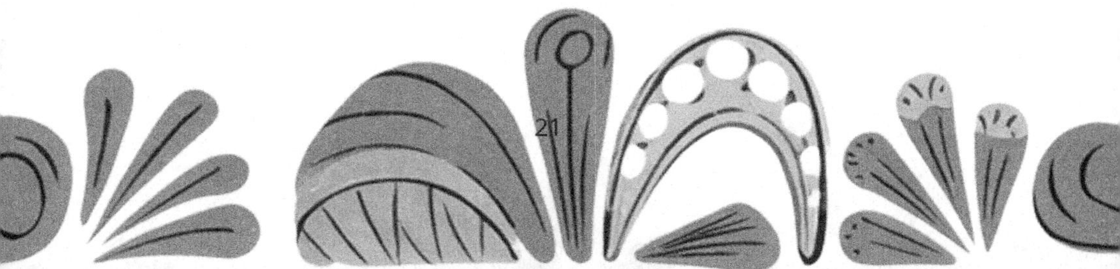

STRENGTHENING YOUR IDENTITY IN CHRIST

In a world that constantly tells you who you should be, it's easy to feel lost or unsure of yourself. This chapter helps you find your true identity in Christ. You'll explore what it means to be "fearfully and wonderfully made," embrace the confidence that comes from knowing God's purpose for your life, and learn how to overcome doubts and negative thoughts. By the end of this chapter, you'll be ready to live boldly as the person God created you to be.

WEEK 5

You Are Fearfully and Wonderfully Made

"I praise You because I am fearfully and wonderfully made; Your works are wonderful, I know that full well."
– Psalm 139:14

REFLECTION

It's easy to compare yourself to others, especially in a world filled with social media and constant opinions. But this verse reminds you of something powerful: you are intentionally and beautifully created by God. Every part of who you are—your strengths, talents, and even your struggles—was made with care and purpose. Embracing this truth allows you to see yourself the way God sees you: as His masterpiece. You don't need to be perfect, because God has already made you enough.

WEEKLY CHALLENGE

Write down three things you love about yourself and thank God for each of them. If you find this difficult, pray for God to help you see yourself through His eyes. At the end of the week, reflect on how this practice changes your self-perception.

Share your thoughts:

JOURNAL QUESTIONS

What is one thing about yourself that you love and want to thank God for?

How does knowing that God created you with purpose make you feel?

How can you use your unique talents to honor God?

WEEK 6

Finding Your Purpose Through Faith

"For I know the plans I have for you," declares the Lord, "plans to prosper you and not to harm you, plans to give you hope and a future." – Jeremiah 29:11

REFLECTION

Sometimes life can feel directionless or overwhelming, especially when you're unsure of what lies ahead. But this verse reminds you that God already has a plan for your life. It's a plan filled with hope, purpose, and meaning. You don't have to figure everything out right now; instead, focus on trusting God and taking one step at a time. When you rely on Him, you'll begin to discover the incredible purpose He has for you.

WEEKLY CHALLENGE

Spend some time this week praying about your future. Write down one area of your life where you're seeking clarity or direction, and ask God to guide you. At the end of the week, write down any insights or peace you've gained from trusting Him.

Share your thoughts:

PRAYER TIPS

1 Pray and ask God to show you His plan for your life.

2 Look for clues in your interests and passions—they often align with your purpose.

3 Trust that God's timing is perfect, even if His plans don't unfold right away.

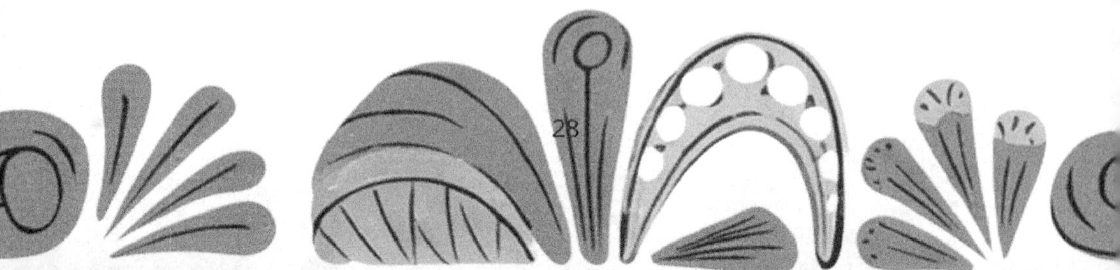

WEEK 7

Overcoming Doubts About Who You Are

"But you are a chosen people, a royal priesthood, a holy nation, God's special possession, that you may declare the praises of Him who called you out of darkness into His wonderful light." – 1 Peter 2:9

REFLECTION

Doubts about your worth or identity can creep in, especially when you face criticism or failure. But this verse is a powerful reminder of who you are in God's eyes. You are chosen, loved, and set apart for a purpose. God calls you His "special possession," meaning you have immense value. When you start to doubt yourself, turn to God's truth instead of the world's opinions.

WEEKLY CHALLENGE

This week, write down three Bible verses that remind you of your identity in Christ (starting with 1 Peter 2:9). Whenever you feel doubt creeping in, read these verses aloud and reflect on their meaning. Notice how this practice helps you push through negative thoughts..

Share your thoughts:

JOURNAL QUESTIONS

What doubts do you struggle with most about yourself?

How does knowing God calls you His special possession (1 Peter 2:9) change the way you see yourself?

What steps can you take to remind yourself of your identity in Christ?

WEEK 8

Embracing Confidence in Christ

"I can do all this through Him who gives me strength." – Philippians 4:13

REFLECTION

True confidence doesn't come from achievements, popularity, or possessions. It comes from knowing that God is with you every step of the way. This verse reminds you that with God's strength, you can overcome challenges, face fears, and step boldly into the life He's calling you to live. Confidence in Christ means trusting not only in what He can do through you but also in who He has made you to be.

WEEKLY CHALLENGE

Identify one area of your life where you struggle with confidence—whether it's at school, in sports, or in relationships. This week, pray daily for God to strengthen you in that area. Write down any progress or victories, no matter how small, and thank God for giving you courage.

Share your thoughts:

PRAYER TIPS

1 Repeat this affirmation daily: "I can do all things through Christ who strengthens me."

2 Focus on past moments when God helped you overcome challenges.

3 Surround yourself with friends who encourage your faith and confidence.

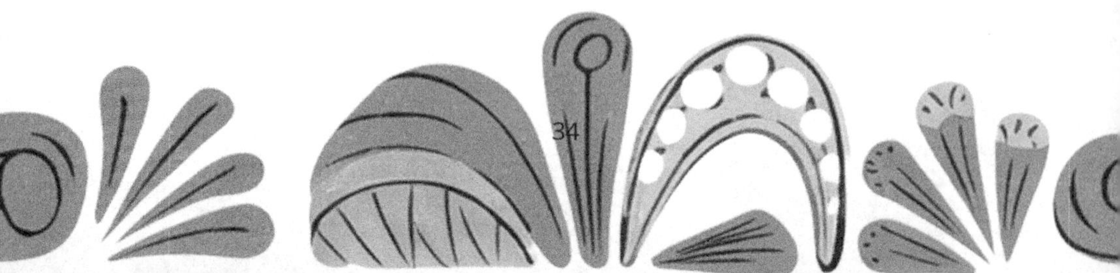

CHAPTER 3

OVERCOMING CHALLENGES THROUGH FAITH

Life is full of challenges—some are small, while others feel overwhelming. This chapter will help you see that God is with you in every trial, giving you the strength and courage to overcome. You'll explore how to trust Him when life feels uncertain, how to turn setbacks into opportunities for growth, and how to face fears with boldness. With God's help, the hardest moments in life can become opportunities to build your faith and grow stronger.

WEEK 9

Trusting God in Uncertain Times

"Trust in the Lord with all your heart and lean not on your own understanding; in all your ways submit to Him, and He will make your paths straight." – Proverbs 3:5-6

REFLECTION

Life is full of uncertainty, and it's natural to want answers and control. But this verse encourages you to lean on God's wisdom, not your own. Trusting God means believing that He has a plan, even when things don't make sense. It's about surrendering your worries and letting Him guide you. When you trust Him fully, He will lead you on the right path, even through difficult or confusing times.

WEEKLY CHALLENGE

Write down one situation in your life where you're feeling uncertain. Each day this week, pray about that situation and ask God to help you trust Him. At the end of the week, reflect on how your trust in God has grown.

Share your thoughts:

JOURNAL QUESTIONS

What's one area of your life where you're struggling to trust God?

How can you remind yourself that God has a plan, even when life feels uncertain?

Who can you talk to when you're feeling overwhelmed or unsure?

WEEK 10

Praying for Strength in Tough Situations

"The Lord is my strength and my shield; my heart trusts in Him, and He helps me. My heart leaps for joy, and with my song I praise Him." – Psalm 28:7

REFLECTION

When life gets hard, it's easy to feel like you're on your own. But this verse reminds you that God is your source of strength. He's not only protecting you but also giving you the energy and courage to keep going. When you pray for strength, you're inviting God to help you handle whatever comes your way. Trusting Him allows you to face challenges with a heart full of hope and joy, knowing that you're not alone.

WEEKLY CHALLENGE

Think about a challenge you're currently facing, whether it's at school, with friends, or at home. Each day this week, pray specifically for strength and guidance in that area. At the end of the week, write down any moments when you felt God's help or encouragement.

Share your thoughts:

PRAYER TIPS

1 Pray specifically for strength when you're feeling weak or overwhelmed.

2 Find and memorize a Bible verse about God's strength (e.g., Psalm 28:7).

3 Share your struggles with a trusted friend or mentor and ask them to pray for you.

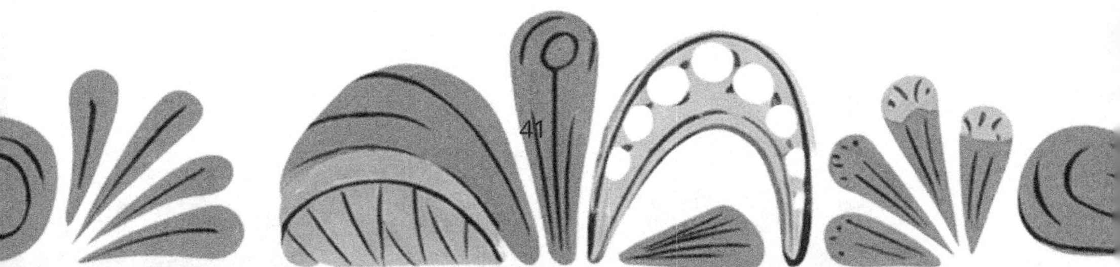

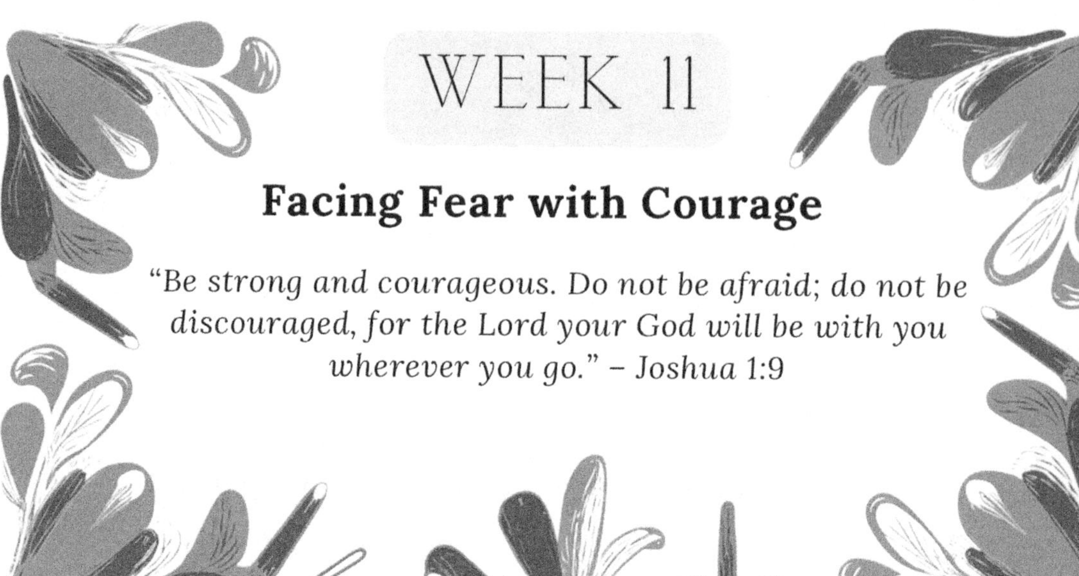

WEEK 11

Facing Fear with Courage

"Be strong and courageous. Do not be afraid; do not be discouraged, for the Lord your God will be with you wherever you go." – Joshua 1:9

REFLECTION

Fear can hold you back from living fully and pursuing your God-given purpose. This verse is a powerful reminder that courage doesn't come from being fearless—it comes from knowing that God is always with you. He's by your side in every situation, giving you the strength to take bold steps of faith. When you trust in God's presence, you can face your fears head-on, knowing you're never alone.

WEEKLY CHALLENGE

Identify one fear or anxiety that's been holding you back. This week, take one small, courageous step toward overcoming it, while praying for God's strength and guidance. Reflect on how taking that step feels and how God supports you through it.

Share your thoughts:

JOURNAL QUESTIONS

What is one fear that's holding you back right now?

How does knowing God is always with you (Joshua 1:9) give you courage?

What's one bold step of faith you can take this week to face your fear?

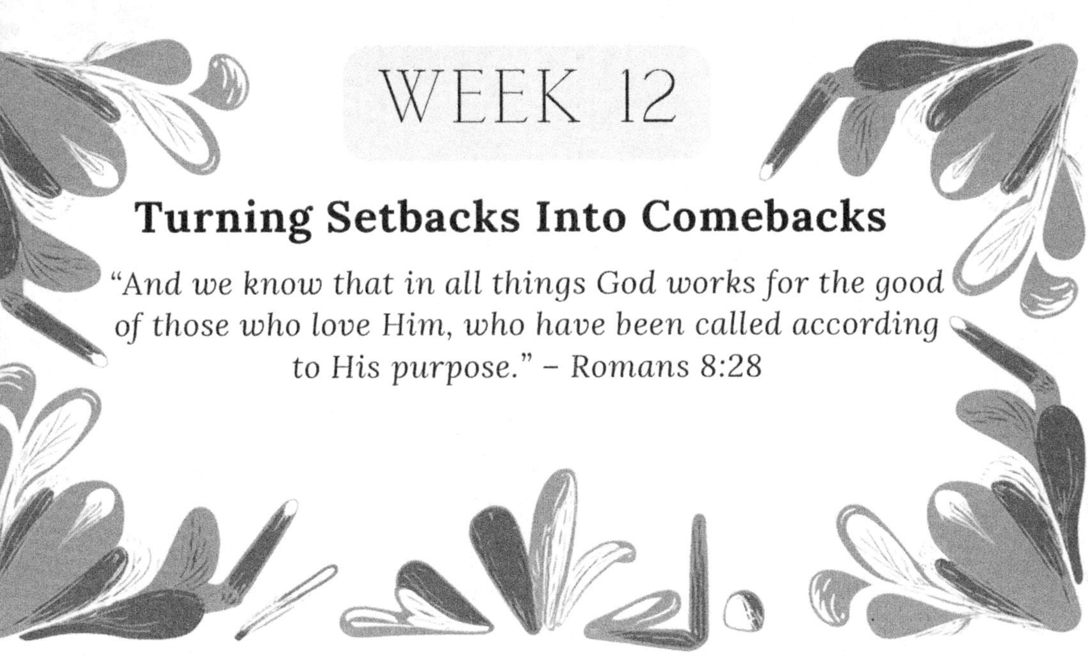

WEEK 12

Turning Setbacks Into Comebacks

"And we know that in all things God works for the good of those who love Him, who have been called according to His purpose." – Romans 8:28

REFLECTION

Setbacks and failures can feel discouraging, but they're not the end of the story. This verse reminds you that God can take even the hardest moments and use them for good. When you trust Him with your struggles, He can turn them into opportunities for growth, strength, and deeper faith. Setbacks aren't a sign of failure—they're a chance to rely on God and let Him work in your life.

WEEKLY CHALLENGE

Think about a recent setback or disappointment you've faced. Write down what you learned from that experience and how God might use it for good. Pray daily for God to help you move forward with hope and trust.

Share your thoughts:

PRAYER TIPS

1 Reflect on a setback you've faced and how it's helped you grow stronger.

2 Remember that failures don't define you—God uses them to build your faith.

3 Pray for wisdom to see the lessons in every challenge.

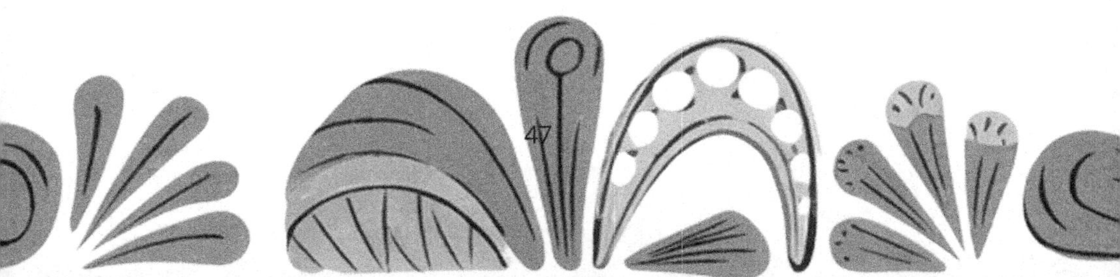

CHAPTER 4

BUILDING STRONG RELATIONSHIPS

Healthy relationships are key to living a fulfilling life, and God cares deeply about how you treat the people around you. This chapter will guide you through becoming a faithful friend, navigating peer pressure, forgiving others, and strengthening family bonds. You'll learn how prayer and God's wisdom can transform your relationships, helping you to love others well and build meaningful connections that reflect God's love.

WEEK 13

Being a Faithful Friend

"A friend loves at all times, and a brother is born for a time of adversity." – Proverbs 17:17

REFLECTION

Friendship is one of God's gifts, but being a faithful friend takes effort and intentionality. This verse reminds us of the importance of love and loyalty, especially during tough times. True friends support each other, forgive mistakes, and help each other grow. God calls you to be the kind of friend who brings love and encouragement into others' lives.

WEEKLY CHALLENGE

Reach out to a friend who might need encouragement or support. This week, make an effort to check in, offer kind words, or help them with something they're going through. Reflect on how this strengthens your friendship.

Share your thoughts:

JOURNAL QUESTIONS

What qualities do you think make a good friend?

How can you show love and loyalty to your friends this week?

How does God's example of unconditional love inspire you to be a better friend?

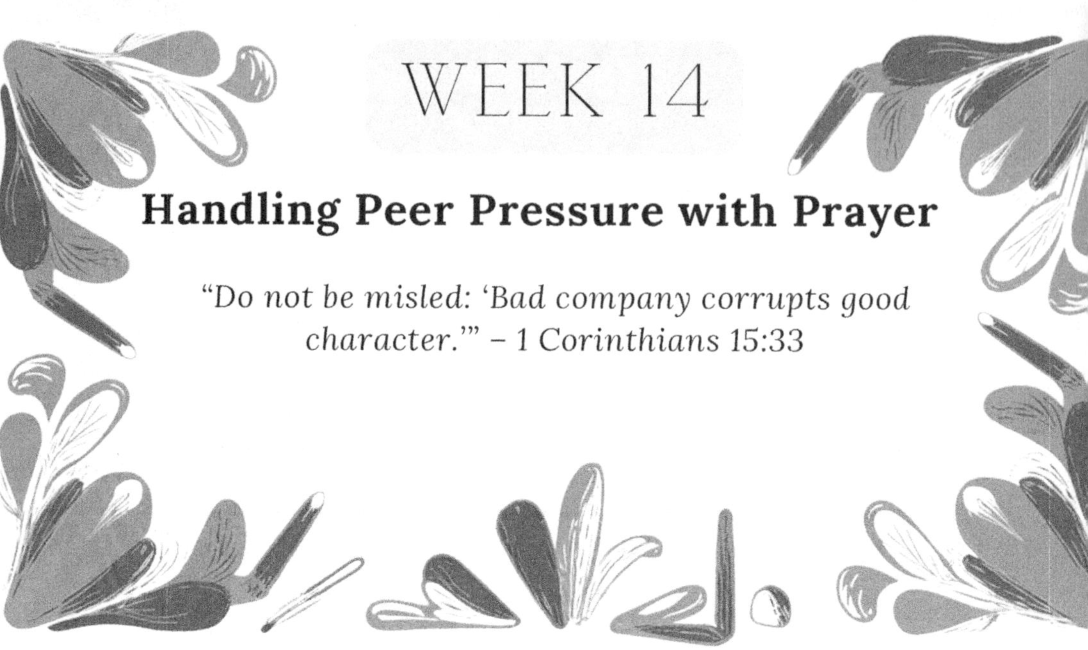

WEEK 14

Handling Peer Pressure with Prayer

"Do not be misled: 'Bad company corrupts good character.'" – 1 Corinthians 15:33

REFLECTION

Peer pressure can lead you to make choices that don't align with your values. This verse warns us to be careful about the people we surround ourselves with. Prayer can help you stand firm in your beliefs and give you the strength to say no when others try to steer you in the wrong direction. Trust that God will guide you toward friendships that help you grow.

WEEKLY CHALLENGE

Think about one situation where you've faced peer pressure or felt tempted to compromise your values. Pray daily for strength to make the right choices, and write down how God helps you stand firm this week.

Share your thoughts:

PRAYER TIPS

1. Pray for strength before entering situations where you feel pressured.

2. Remember: Saying "no" to something wrong is saying "yes" to God.

3. Surround yourself with friends who respect your values and encourage your faith.

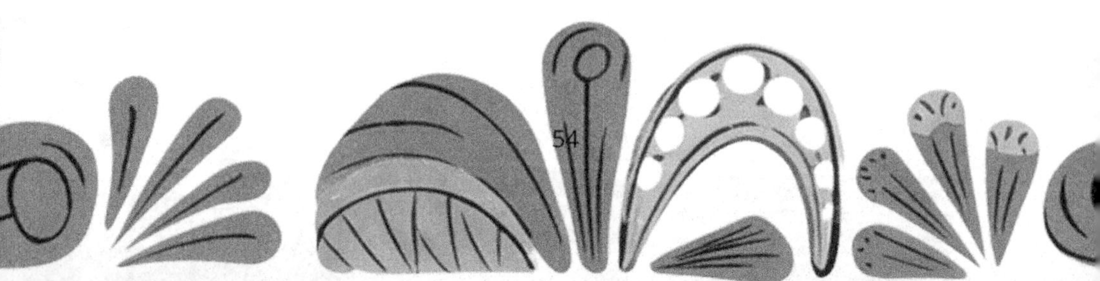

WEEK 15

Forgiving Others as Christ Forgives You

"Bear with each other and forgive one another if any of you has a grievance against someone. Forgive as the Lord forgave you." – Colossians 3:13

REFLECTION

Forgiveness can be one of the hardest things to offer, especially when someone has hurt you deeply. But this verse reminds us that just as Christ forgave us, we are called to forgive others. Forgiveness isn't about letting someone off the hook—it's about freeing your heart from anger and bitterness. When you choose forgiveness, you allow God to bring healing and peace into your relationships.

WEEKLY CHALLENGE

Identify someone you've been holding a grudge against. Spend this week praying for the strength to forgive them. Write down your thoughts about how forgiveness impacts your heart and your relationship with God.

Share your thoughts:

JOURNAL QUESTIONS

Is there someone in your life you need to forgive? Why is it hard?

How does remembering God's forgiveness toward you help you forgive others?

What steps can you take this week to let go of anger or resentment?

WEEK 16

Strengthening Family Bonds Through Prayer

"Honor your father and your mother, so that you may live long in the land the Lord your God is giving you." – Exodus 20:12

REFLECTION

Family relationships can sometimes feel challenging, but they are an important part of God's plan for your life. This verse encourages you to honor and respect your parents and family members. Prayer can help you approach your family with patience, love, and understanding, even when conflicts arise. God wants to strengthen your family bonds and bring peace to your home.

WEEKLY CHALLENGE

Pray for each member of your family this week, asking God to bless them and strengthen your relationship with them. Write down one way you can show love or respect to your family, and make an effort to act on it.

Share your thoughts:

PRAYER TIPS

1 Pray for each member of your family by name and ask God to bless them.

2 Make time to listen and show kindness to a family member this week.

3 Use prayer to invite God into any family conflicts or challenges.

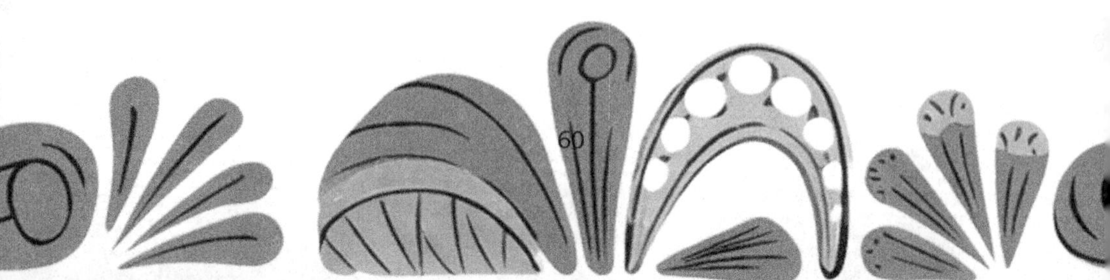

CHAPTER 5

FINDING PEACE IN A BUSY WORLD

The world is loud, busy, and sometimes overwhelming—but God offers a peace that goes beyond understanding. This chapter focuses on slowing down to hear God's voice, managing stress through prayer, letting go of worry, and experiencing peace in every moment. You'll discover that peace isn't about having a perfect life—it's about trusting God, even when things feel chaotic. By applying these lessons, you can create space for God's peace in your everyday life.

WEEK 17

Slowing Down to Hear God's Voice

"Be still, and know that I am God." – Psalm 46:10

REFLECTION

In today's fast-paced world, it's easy to feel overwhelmed by noise and distractions. This verse invites you to slow down and be still in God's presence. When you take time to quiet your mind and heart, you can hear God's voice more clearly. Slowing down allows you to connect with Him and find the peace you're searching for.

WEEKLY CHALLENGE

Set aside 10 minutes each day this week to sit in silence with God. No phones, no distractions—just you and Him. Reflect on how this time of stillness impacts your mindset and your connection with God.

Share your thoughts:

JOURNAL QUESTIONS

When was the last time you felt God speaking to you?

What distractions keep you from hearing God's voice?

How can you create more quiet moments to connect with Him this week?

WEEK 18

Managing Stress Through Prayer

"Cast all your anxiety on Him because He cares for you."
– 1 Peter 5:7

REFLECTION

Stress can feel like a heavy burden, but this verse reminds you that you don't have to carry it alone. God cares deeply about you and invites you to give your worries to Him. Prayer is a way to release your stress and trust that God is in control. When you pray about your anxieties, you'll find that God gives you the peace and strength to handle them.

WEEKLY CHALLENGE

Each day this week, write down one thing that's causing you stress. Pray about it and ask God to help you release it into His hands. At the end of the week, reflect on how you feel after surrendering your stress to Him.

Share your thoughts:

PRAYER TIPS

1 When you feel stressed, stop and take a deep breath while saying a short prayer.

2 Write down your worries and give them to God through prayer.

3 Take breaks from screens and spend a few minutes in quiet reflection with God.

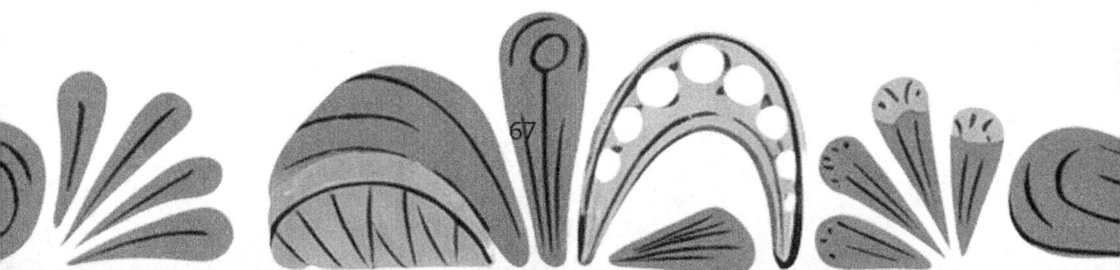

WEEK 19

Letting Go of Worry

"Therefore do not worry about tomorrow, for tomorrow will worry about itself. Each day has enough trouble of its own." – Matthew 6:34

REFLECTION

Worrying about the future can rob you of the joy and peace that God wants you to experience today. This verse reminds you to live in the present and trust God with the days ahead. God already knows your future, and He promises to provide for you every step of the way.

WEEKLY CHALLENGE

This week, practice living in the present. When you catch yourself worrying about the future, stop and pray. Write down how focusing on today helps you feel more peace and trust in God.

Share your thoughts:

JOURNAL QUESTIONS

What is one worry that keeps you up at night?

How can trusting God's plan help you let go of your anxiety?

What Bible verse about peace can you memorize to remind yourself not to worry?

WEEK 20

Seeking God's Peace in Every Moment

"The peace of God, which transcends all understanding, will guard your hearts and your minds in Christ Jesus."
– Philippians 4:7

REFLECTION

God's peace is different from anything the world can offer—it's a peace that doesn't depend on circumstances. This verse reminds you that when you trust in Christ, His peace will protect your heart and mind from fear, worry, and chaos. Seeking God's peace means turning to Him in prayer and trusting Him, no matter what you're facing.

WEEKLY CHALLENGE

At the end of each day, write down one moment when you felt peace and one moment when you felt stressed or overwhelmed. Pray about both, asking God to help you experience His peace more consistently.

Share your thoughts:

PRAYER TIPS

1 Whenever you feel overwhelmed, say, "God, I trust You to handle this."

2 Spend time outdoors and thank God for the beauty around you.

3 Keep a gratitude list to focus on what God has done in your life.

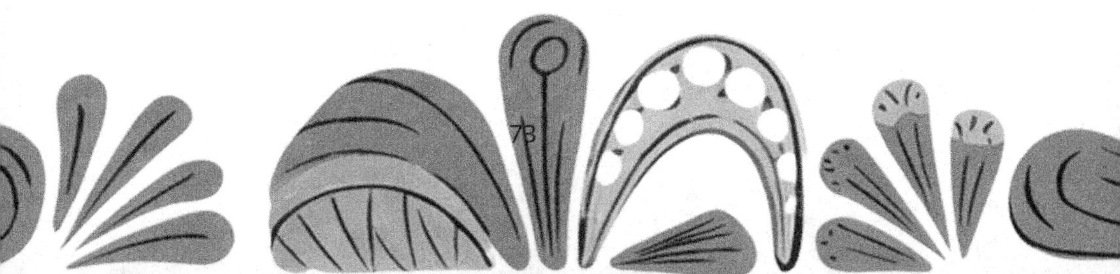

CHAPTER 6

DEVELOPING GODLY WISDOM

Wisdom is more than knowledge—it's about making decisions that honor God and align with His plans for your life. In this chapter, you'll learn how to seek wisdom through Scripture, look to biblical heroes as examples, and rely on God's guidance in tough decisions. Wisdom is a gift that grows as you follow God's Word, and this chapter will equip you to make choices that lead to a life of faith and purpose.

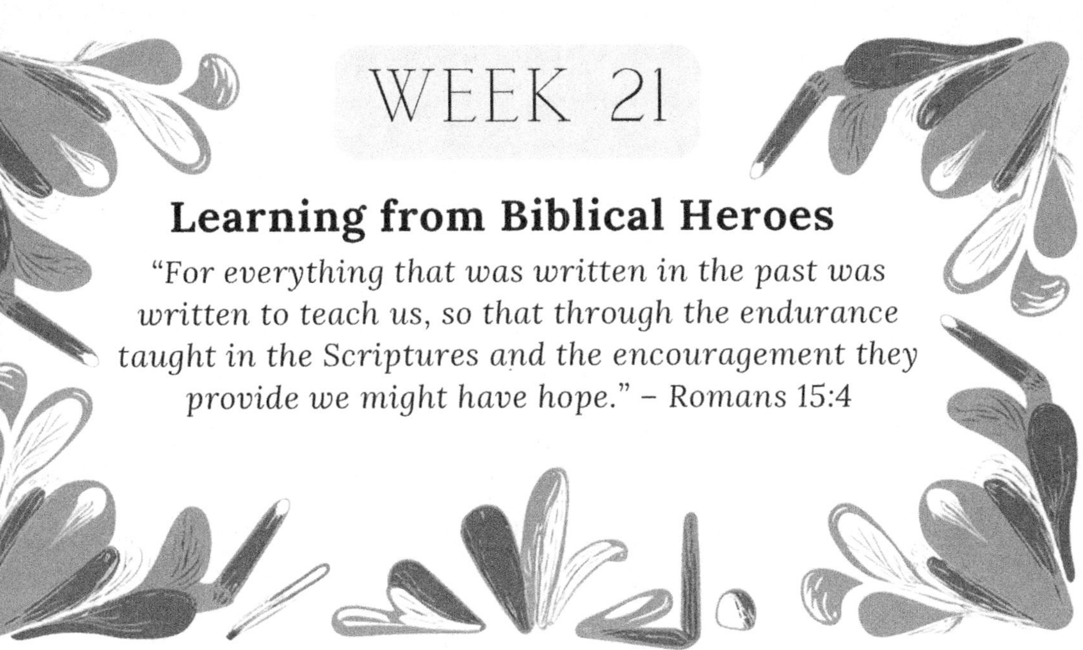

WEEK 21

Learning from Biblical Heroes

"For everything that was written in the past was written to teach us, so that through the endurance taught in the Scriptures and the encouragement they provide we might have hope." – Romans 15:4

REFLECTION

The Bible is full of stories about ordinary people who trusted God and accomplished extraordinary things. These stories aren't just history—they're lessons for you today. By studying the lives of biblical heroes, you can learn about faith, courage, and perseverance. Their victories and struggles can inspire you to follow God's path in your own life.

WEEKLY CHALLENGE

Choose one biblical hero (e.g., David, Esther, Joseph) and read their story this week. Write down three lessons you learn from their life and how you can apply them to your own journey.

Share your thoughts:

JOURNAL QUESTIONS

Who is your favorite biblical hero, and why?

What qualities did they show that you admire and want to develop?

How can their story encourage you to trust God in your own life?

WEEK 22

Making Wise Decisions in School and Life

"If any of you lacks wisdom, you should ask God, who gives generously to all without finding fault, and it will be given to you." – James 1:5

REFLECTION

Life is full of decisions, big and small. This verse reminds you that you don't have to figure everything out on your own. God offers His wisdom to help guide your choices—you just need to ask Him. Whether it's deciding how to spend your time, who to hang out with, or what direction to take in your life, prayer and trust in God's wisdom can help you stay on the right path.

WEEKLY CHALLENGE

Think about a decision you need to make this week. Pray each day for God to guide you. Write down any insights or peace you feel as you seek His wisdom and take one step toward making that decision with His help.

Share your thoughts:

PRAYER TIPS

1. Pray before making any major decisions and ask for God's wisdom.

2. Write out the pros and cons of your choices and see how they align with God's Word.

3. Talk to a trusted mentor or parent when you're unsure about a decision.

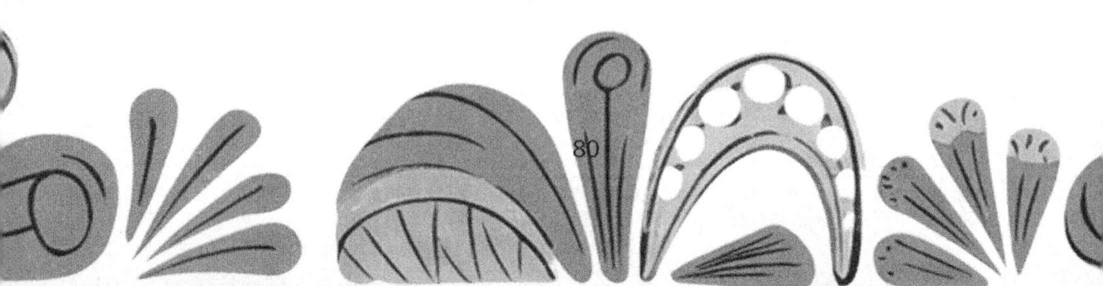

WEEK 23

Recognizing God's Guidance

"Whether you turn to the right or to the left, your ears will hear a voice behind you, saying, 'This is the way; walk in it.'" - Isaiah 30:21

REFLECTION

God's guidance isn't always loud or obvious—it often comes in quiet whispers, nudges, or moments of clarity. This verse is a reminder that God is always ready to lead you, even when you're unsure of which way to go. By paying attention to His voice through prayer, Scripture, and the wisdom of others, you can trust that He will direct your steps.

WEEKLY CHALLENGE

Take a few minutes each day to ask God for direction in a specific area of your life. Write down any feelings, thoughts, or Scriptures that come to mind and reflect on how God might be guiding you.

Share your thoughts:

JOURNAL QUESTIONS

How has God guided you in the past, even when you didn't realize it at the time?

What is one area where you're seeking His direction right now?

How can you stay open to God's leading, even if it's not what you expected?

WEEK 24

Turning Mistakes Into Lessons

"The righteous may fall seven times, but they rise again."
– Proverbs 24:16

REFLECTION

Mistakes and failures are part of life, but they don't have to hold you back. This verse reminds you that what matters is not how many times you fall, but how you get back up with God's help. Each mistake is an opportunity to learn, grow, and rely on God's grace. When you turn to Him, He can use even your failures to shape you into the person He's calling you to be.

WEEKLY CHALLENGE

Think of a recent mistake or failure. Write about what you learned from it and how God can use it for good. Pray for strength and wisdom to keep moving forward, trusting that God is helping you grow.

Share your thoughts:

PRAYER TIPS

1. Remember: Mistakes don't define you—God uses them to help you grow.

2. Pray for the wisdom to see the lessons in your mistakes.

3. Write down one thing you learned from a past mistake and how it helped you grow stronger.

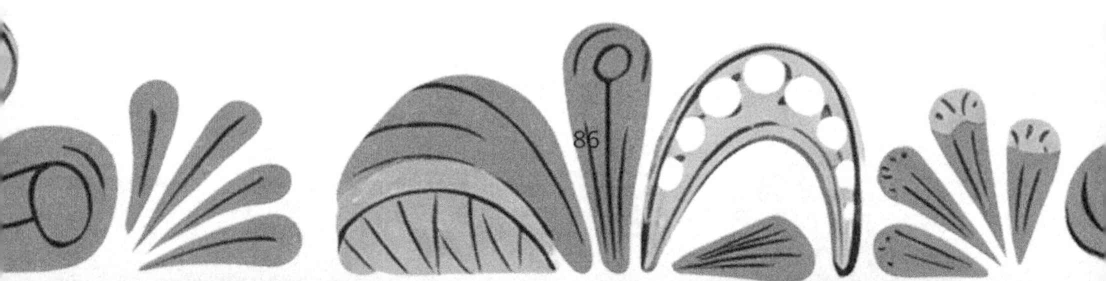

CHAPTER 7

LIVING OUT YOUR FAITH

Your faith isn't just something you believe—it's something you live out every day. This chapter will help you become a light in the world by reflecting God's love and truth in your actions. You'll explore how to confidently share your faith, serve others with love, and stand firm in your beliefs, even when it's challenging. Living out your faith is about letting your relationship with God shape every part of your life, so others can see His power at work in you.

WEEK 25

Being a Light in the World

"You are the light of the world. A town built on a hill cannot be hidden." – Matthew 5:14

REFLECTION

Jesus calls you to be a light—a positive influence in the world. Being a light means reflecting God's love, kindness, and truth through your words and actions. It's not about being perfect but about living in a way that points others to God. Even small acts of kindness can shine brightly in a world that often feels dark.

WEEKLY CHALLENGE

This week, perform one intentional act of kindness each day—whether it's helping someone, offering encouragement, or standing up for what's right. Write down how these actions make you feel and how others respond.

Share your thoughts:

JOURNAL QUESTIONS

What does it mean to you to "be a light" in the world?

How can you show God's love to someone who's struggling this week?

How does your faith inspire others to live with hope and purpose?

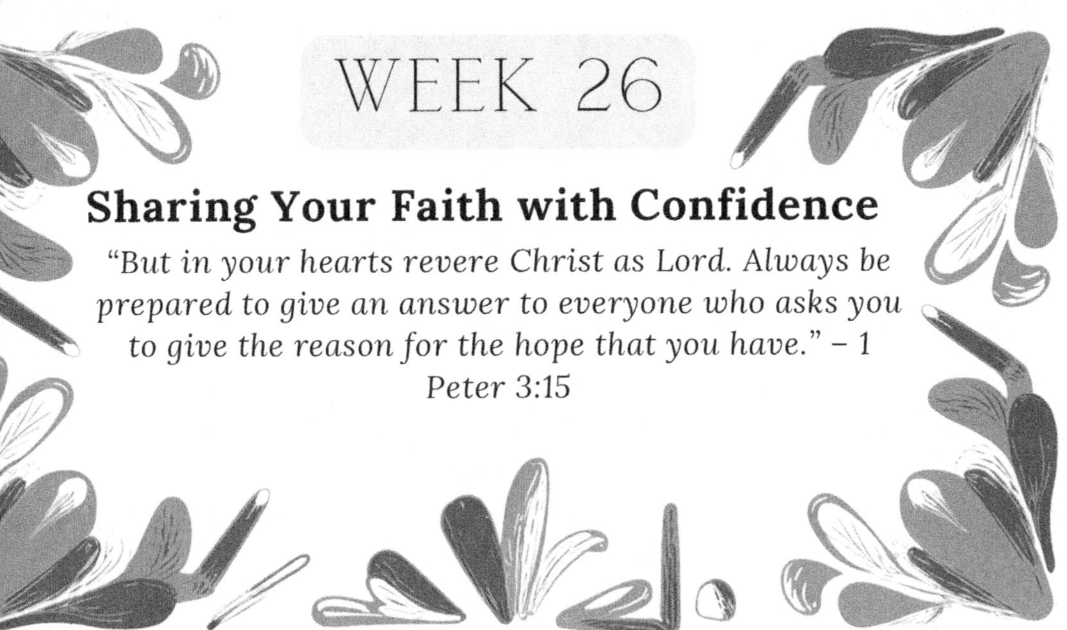

WEEK 26

Sharing Your Faith with Confidence

"But in your hearts revere Christ as Lord. Always be prepared to give an answer to everyone who asks you to give the reason for the hope that you have." – 1 Peter 3:15

REFLECTION

Sharing your faith doesn't mean having all the answers—it means being willing to talk about what God has done in your life. This verse encourages you to share your hope in Christ with humility and confidence. Your story can inspire others to explore their own faith, and God will give you the words to say when the time comes.

WEEKLY CHALLENGE

Think of one person you can share your faith with this week. It could be through a conversation, a kind gesture, or inviting them to church. Reflect on how sharing your hope in Christ impacts both you and them.

Share your thoughts:

PRAYER TIPS

1. Share your story of how God has worked in your life—it's powerful!

2. Pray for courage before talking about your faith with someone.

3. Listen to others' questions or doubts with kindness and honesty.

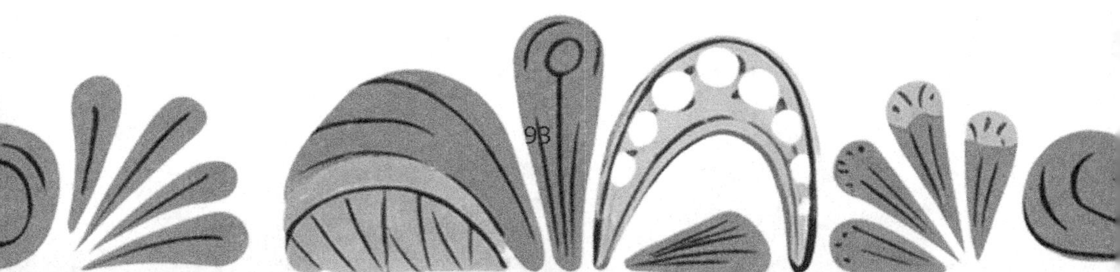

WEEK 27

Serving Others in Love

"Each of you should use whatever gift you have received to serve others, as faithful stewards of God's grace in its various forms." – 1 Peter 4:10

REFLECTION

God has given you unique gifts and talents, and He calls you to use them to serve others. Serving in love is an act of worship and a way to show others God's grace. Whether it's helping a friend, volunteering, or encouraging someone, your actions reflect God's love and make a difference in the lives of those around you.

WEEKLY CHALLENGE

This week, find one way to use your gifts to serve someone else. Write about how serving makes you feel and how it strengthens your connection with God.

Share your thoughts:

JOURNAL QUESTIONS

Who is someone in your life that you can serve this week?

How does serving others help you grow closer to God?

What gifts or talents can you use to make a difference in someone's life?

WEEK 28

Standing Firm in Your Beliefs

"Be on your guard; stand firm in the faith; be courageous; be strong." – 1 Corinthians 16:13

REFLECTION

Standing firm in your beliefs isn't always easy, especially when others challenge your faith. This verse reminds you to stay strong and courageous, trusting God to help you stay true to Him. Standing firm doesn't mean being argumentative—it means being confident in what you believe and showing love and grace in how you live your life.

WEEKLY CHALLENGE

Think of one situation where it's hard to stand firm in your faith. Pray for strength and wisdom to handle it well. Write down any progress or victories you experience this week.

Share your thoughts:

PRAYER TIPS

1. Memorize a Bible verse that strengthens your confidence in your beliefs.

2. Practice saying “no” to things that go against your faith, even in small situations.

3. Pray for courage to stand firm, even when others don’t understand your choices.

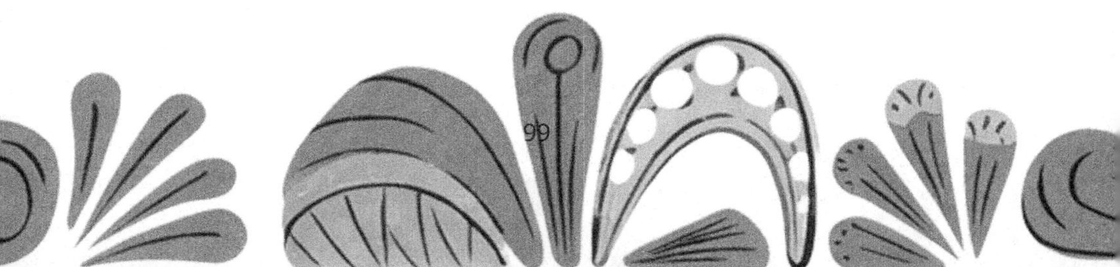

CHAPTER 8

GROWING SPIRITUALLY THROUGH CHALLENGES

Challenges can feel discouraging, but they're also opportunities for spiritual growth. This chapter shows you how to find strength in weakness, trust God when life feels unfair, and overcome temptation with prayer. God doesn't waste your struggles—He uses them to build your character, deepen your faith, and draw you closer to Him. By the end of this chapter, you'll see challenges not as obstacles but as stepping stones to a stronger relationship with God.

WEEK 29

Finding Strength in Weakness

"But He said to me, 'My grace is sufficient for you, for My power is made perfect in weakness.'" – 2 Corinthians 12:9

REFLECTION

It's natural to want to avoid weakness, but this verse shows that God's power is greatest when we depend on Him. When you feel weak, it's an opportunity to lean on God and experience His strength working through you. Your struggles are not signs of failure—they are chances to grow closer to God and see His grace in action.

WEEKLY CHALLENGE

Write down one area of your life where you feel weak. Each day this week, pray for God's strength and guidance in that area. Reflect on how He shows up in your moments of need.

Share your thoughts:

JOURNAL QUESTIONS

What is one area where you feel weak or not good enough?

How does God's promise in 2 Corinthians 12:9 give you hope?

How can you rely on God's strength when you face challenges this week?

WEEK 30

Trusting God When Life Feels Unfair

"The Lord is righteous in all His ways and faithful in all He does." – Psalm 145:17

REFLECTION

Life doesn't always feel fair, and it's easy to question why bad things happen. This verse reminds you that God is always faithful and just, even when life feels unfair. Trusting Him means believing that He sees the bigger picture and is working for your good, even in difficult times.

WEEKLY CHALLENGE

Identify one situation where life feels unfair. Pray about it every day this week, asking God to help you trust Him and see His faithfulness. Write down any ways you notice His presence in the situation.

Share your thoughts:

PRAYER TIPS

1 Remember that God sees the bigger picture, even when things seem unfair.

2 Pray for patience and wisdom in tough situations.

3 Look for ways God might be using the situation to grow your character.

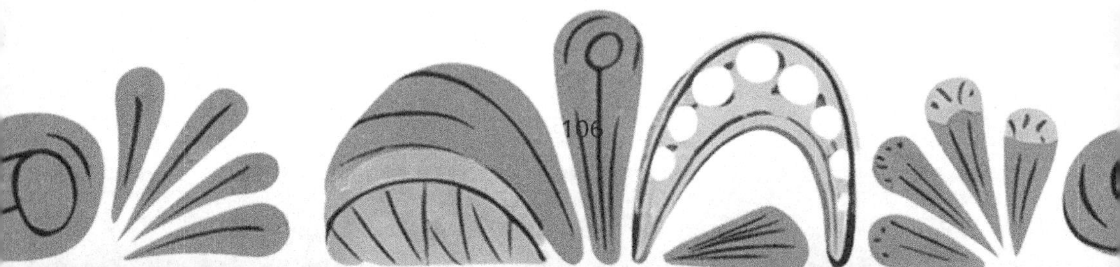

WEEK 31

Staying Faithful Through Hard Times

"Blessed is the one who perseveres under trial because, having stood the test, that person will receive the crown of life that the Lord has promised to those who love Him." – James 1:12

REFLECTION

Hard times are a part of life, but this verse reminds you that staying faithful during trials is worth it. God sees your perseverance and promises blessings for those who remain steadfast. It's not about pretending everything is fine but about trusting that God is with you, even when things feel overwhelming. Faith grows stronger when it's tested, and God uses your challenges to shape you into who He's called you to be.

WEEKLY CHALLENGE

Think about a challenge you're facing right now. Each day this week, write a short prayer asking God for strength to stay faithful. At the end of the week, reflect on how trusting God has impacted your attitude and perseverance.

Share your thoughts:

JOURNAL QUESTIONS

What is one challenge you're currently facing where you need God's help?

____

____

____

How can trusting God's promises help you stay faithful during difficult times?

____

____

____

What are some ways you've seen God work in your life during past struggles?

____

____

____

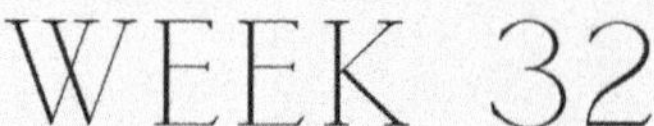

WEEK 32

Overcoming Temptation with Prayer

"No temptation has overtaken you except what is common to mankind. And God is faithful; He will not let you be tempted beyond what you can bear. But when you are tempted, He will also provide a way out so that you can endure it." – 1 Corinthians 10:13

REFLECTION

Everyone faces temptation, and this verse reminds you that you're not alone in the struggle. God is faithful and always provides a way to resist temptation if you rely on Him. Overcoming temptation starts with prayer—asking God for strength and looking for the "way out" He promises. With His help, you can say no to things that pull you away from Him and yes to the life He has planned for you.

WEEKLY CHALLENGE

Identify one area of your life where you face temptation. Pray daily this week for God to help you resist it and for wisdom to see the way out. Write down any victories, big or small, that God helps you achieve in overcoming temptation.

Share your thoughts:

PRAYER TIPS

1. When you feel tempted, pause and pray immediately for God's help to resist.

2. Find a trusted friend or mentor to talk to about your struggles and ask them to pray for you.

3. Replace the temptation with something positive—for example, read Scripture or listen to worship music when you feel tempted.

CHAPTER 9

DREAMING BIG WITH GOD

God has incredible plans for your life, and He's ready to walk with you as you pursue your dreams. This chapter will help you discover your God-given talents, set goals that align with His purpose, trust His timing, and take bold steps of faith. Dreaming with God isn't just about achieving success—it's about letting Him shape your vision and guide your steps so that your life becomes a reflection of His glory.

WEEK 33

Discovering Your God-Given Talents

"For we are God's handiwork, created in Christ Jesus to do good works, which God prepared in advance for us to do." – Ephesians 2:10

REFLECTION

God has given you unique talents and abilities for a reason. This verse reminds you that you are created for good works—specific tasks that only you can do. Discovering your God-given talents is about recognizing the gifts He's placed in you and using them to make a difference in the world.

WEEKLY CHALLENGE

Make a list of your talents, interests, and strengths. Pray about how you can use them to honor God and serve others. Write down any ideas or opportunities that come to mind.

Share your thoughts:

JOURNAL QUESTIONS

What is one skill or talent you're proud of, and how do you think God wants you to use it?

____

____

____

How can your talents reflect God's glory and love to others?

____

____

____

Who has encouraged or inspired you to embrace your gifts, and how can you thank them?

____

____

____

WEEK 34

Setting Faith-Filled Goals

"Commit to the Lord whatever you do, and He will establish your plans." – Proverbs 16:3

REFLECTION

Setting goals is important, but this verse reminds us to invite God into our plans. Faith-filled goals are those that align with His purpose for your life. When you commit your goals to God, He will guide you and give you the wisdom to pursue them.

WEEKLY CHALLENGE

Set one goal for yourself this week—whether it's spiritual, academic, or personal. Pray about it and ask God for guidance. Write down steps you can take to work toward it and reflect on your progress.

Share your thoughts:

PRAYER TIPS

1 Pray before setting any goals and ask God to align your dreams with His plan for your life.

2 Break your goals into small, actionable steps that you can work on daily or weekly.

3 Write your goals somewhere visible and pray over them regularly, trusting God to guide you.

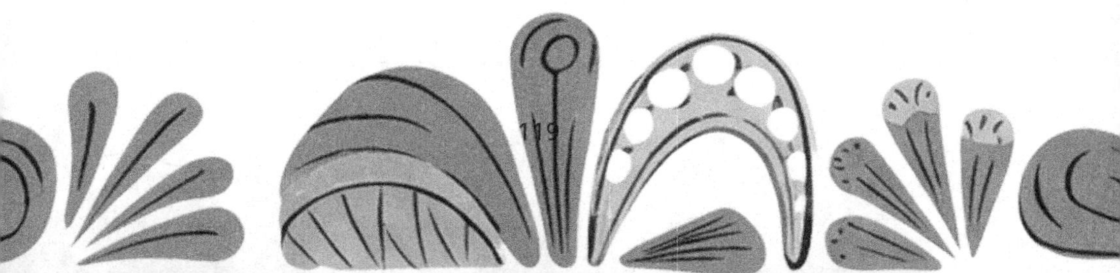

WEEK 35

Trusting God's Timing for Your Dreams

"There is a time for everything, and a season for every activity under the heavens." – Ecclesiastes 3:1

REFLECTION

It can be hard to wait for your dreams to come true, especially when you want answers right now. But this verse reminds you that God's timing is perfect. He knows the best time to bring your dreams to life, even if it feels like you're waiting forever. Trusting His timing allows you to grow in patience, faith, and preparation while you wait for His plans to unfold.

WEEKLY CHALLENGE

Think about one dream or goal where you're struggling to trust God's timing. Pray about it each day this week, asking God to give you patience and faith. Write down how trusting His timing changes your perspective.

Share your thoughts:

JOURNAL QUESTIONS

What's one thing you're waiting for God to do in your life?

How can trusting God's timing bring you peace instead of frustration?

What steps can you take to prepare for the dream God has placed on your heart?

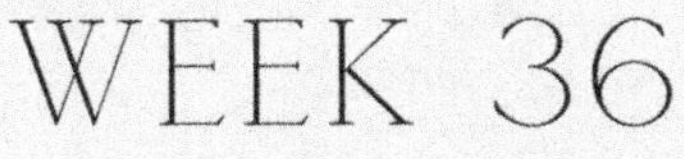

WEEK 36

Taking Bold Steps of Faith

"Be strong and courageous. Do not be afraid; do not be discouraged, for the Lord your God will be with you wherever you go." – Joshua 1:9

REFLECTION

Faith often requires action, even when you feel nervous or unsure. This verse reminds you that God is always with you, giving you the strength to take bold steps of faith. Whether it's pursuing a dream, sharing your faith, or stepping out of your comfort zone, you can move forward with courage because God is by your side

WEEKLY CHALLENGE

Identify one bold step you can take this week to grow in your faith—whether it's helping someone, sharing your story, or starting something new. Pray for courage and take that step, trusting God to lead you.

Share your thoughts:

PRAYER TIPS

1. Pray for courage before taking action—remind yourself that God is with you.

2. Start small if you feel overwhelmed; even small acts of faith can make a big difference.

3. Share your step of faith with someone you trust for encouragement and accountability.

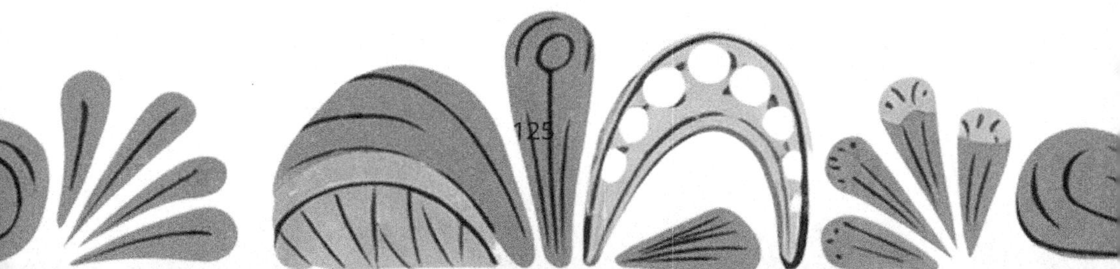

CHAPTER 10

GRATITUDE AND CONTENTMENT

True joy doesn't come from what you have —it comes from a heart that's full of gratitude and contentment in God. In this chapter, you'll learn to appreciate the small blessings in your life, cultivate thankfulness, rely on God's provision, and find peace in all circumstances. Gratitude and contentment are powerful tools that help you focus on God's goodness and experience His joy, no matter what's happening around you.

WEEK 37

Finding Joy in Small Blessings

"This is the day that the Lord has made; let us rejoice and be glad in it." – Psalm 118:24

REFLECTION

Every day is a gift, filled with blessings both big and small. This verse encourages you to find joy in the present moment and celebrate the good things God provides. Gratitude for small blessings can change your perspective and fill your heart with joy, even on tough days.

WEEKLY CHALLENGE

Write down five small blessings you notice each day this week. At the end of the week, reflect on how this practice has helped you feel more joyful and connected to God.

Share your thoughts:

JOURNAL QUESTIONS

What are three small blessings you've noticed today?

How can focusing on small joys help you feel closer to God?

How can you share the joy you've experienced with someone else this week?

WEEK 38

Cultivating a Heart of Thankfulness

"Give thanks in all circumstances; for this is God's will for you in Christ Jesus." – 1 Thessalonians 5:18

REFLECTION

Thankfulness isn't just for when things are going well—it's an attitude you can cultivate in every circumstance. This verse reminds you that gratitude is part of God's plan for your life because it shifts your focus from what's missing to what you already have. A thankful heart brings you closer to God and helps you find joy in everyday moments.

WEEKLY CHALLENGE

Write down three things you're thankful for each day this week. At the end of the week, reflect on how practicing gratitude has impacted your mindset and relationship with God.

Share your thoughts:

PRAYER TIPS

1 Start your prayers with gratitude before asking for anything.

2 Keep a running list of blessings in your journal or on your phone.

3 Find ways to express your thankfulness—whether it's writing a note, saying "thank you," or praying for someone who has blessed you.

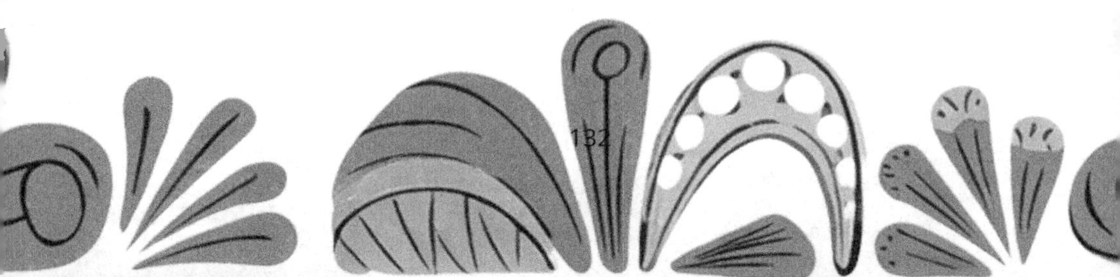

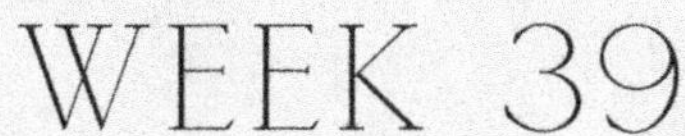

WEEK 39

Relying on God's Provision

"And my God will meet all your needs according to the riches of His glory in Christ Jesus." – Philippians 4:19

REFLECTION

It's easy to worry about having enough—whether it's money, time, or opportunities. This verse reminds you that God knows what you need and promises to provide for you. His provision might not always look the way you expect, but He is faithful to meet your needs in His perfect way. Learning to rely on Him instead of your own strength brings peace and trust.

WEEKLY CHALLENGE

Think of an area in your life where you're worried about having enough—whether it's time, energy, or resources. Pray each day this week, asking God to provide for your needs. Write down any ways you notice His provision during the week.

Share your thoughts:

JOURNAL QUESTIONS

When you're worried about a need, pray instead of stressing—trust that God will provide.

Reflect on past times when God met your needs and thank Him for His faithfulness.

Practice generosity as a reminder that God's provision is abundant and not limited.

WEEK 40

Learning to Be Content in All Circumstances

"I have learned the secret of being content in any and every situation... I can do all this through Him who gives me strength." – Philippians 4:12-13

REFLECTION

Contentment doesn't mean you stop dreaming or working toward your goals—it means trusting God's presence and plan, no matter where you are right now. This verse shows that true contentment comes from relying on God's strength, not on your circumstances. When you focus on His goodness and provision, you can find peace and joy in every season of life.

WEEKLY CHALLENGE

Identify one area in your life where you feel discontent. Each day this week, pray for God to help you find peace and contentment in that area. Write down how your perspective changes as you rely on His strength.

Share your thoughts:

PRAYER TIPS

1 Focus on what you have instead of what you lack—practice gratitude daily.

2 Avoid comparing yourself to others—God's plan for you is unique and good.

3 Reflect on Philippians 4:12-13 when you feel discontent and pray for God's strength to trust Him.

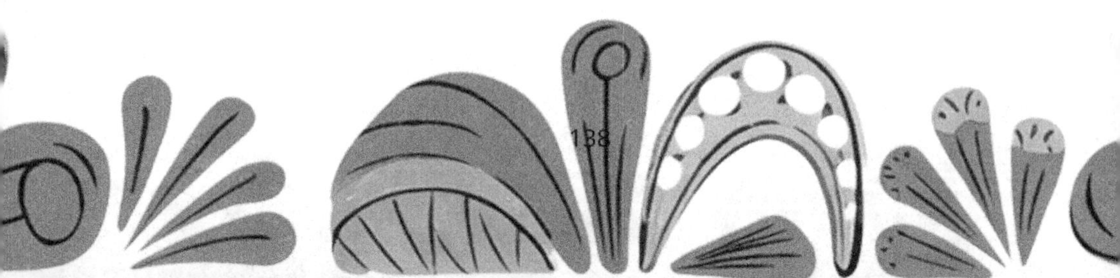

REFLECTING ON YOUR JOURNEY

Reflection is an important part of spiritual growth. This chapter invites you to pause and look back on your faith journey—celebrating victories, learning from challenges, and recognizing how God has worked in your life. It also encourages you to seek His guidance for the next steps in your walk with Him. Reflection isn't just about the past—it's about using what you've learned to keep growing and moving forward in faith.

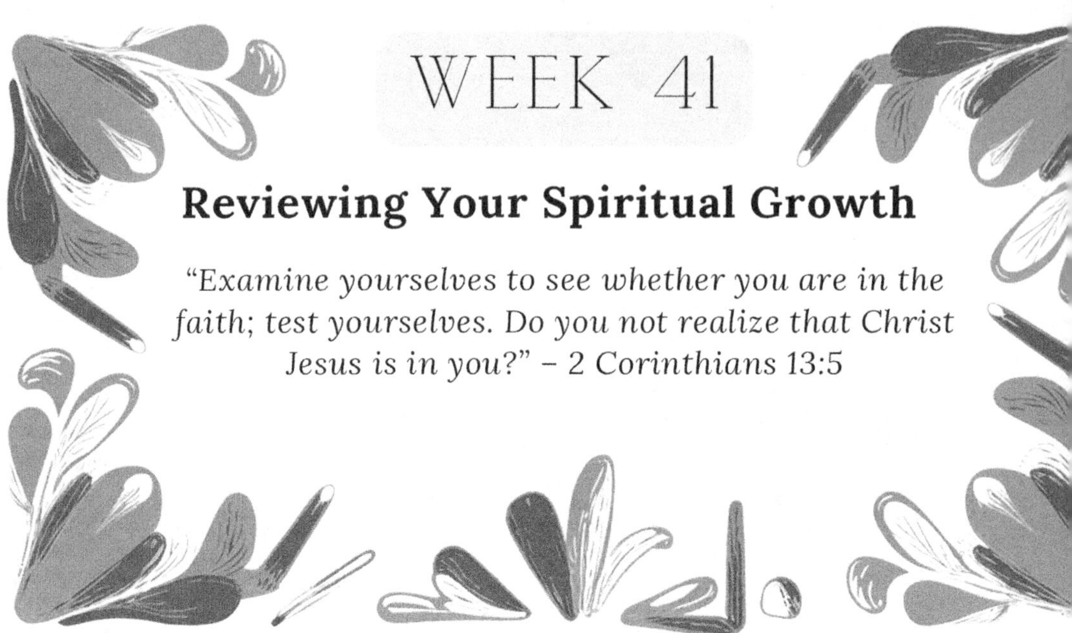

WEEK 41

Reviewing Your Spiritual Growth

"Examine yourselves to see whether you are in the faith; test yourselves. Do you not realize that Christ Jesus is in you?" – 2 Corinthians 13:5

REFLECTION

Taking time to reflect on your spiritual journey helps you see how far you've come and where you can grow further. This verse encourages self-examination—not to criticize yourself, but to recognize how Christ is working in you. By looking back, you can celebrate victories, learn from challenges, and set new goals for your faith.

WEEKLY CHALLENGE

Take a quiet moment each day this week to reflect on your spiritual growth over the past months. Write down one area where you've grown and one area where you want to improve.

Share your thoughts:

JOURNAL QUESTIONS

What's one way your relationship with God has grown over the past year?

How has prayer or reading Scripture changed your perspective on life?

What's one area where you still want to grow spiritually?

WEEK 42

Celebrating Your Victories

"But thanks be to God! He gives us the victory through our Lord Jesus Christ." – 1 Corinthians 15:57

REFLECTION

Every victory in your life—big or small—is a gift from God. This verse reminds you to celebrate these moments and give thanks to the One who makes them possible. Acknowledging your victories not only strengthens your faith but also fills your heart with gratitude and joy.

WEEKLY CHALLENGE

List three victories you've experienced this year. Spend time in prayer thanking God for each one, and write down how these victories have impacted your faith.

Share your thoughts:

PRAYER TIPS

1. Write down three spiritual victories from the past year—big or small—and thank God for them.

2. Share one of your victories with a trusted friend to encourage them in their faith.

3. Plan a small celebration or treat yourself to recognize how far you've come in your journey.

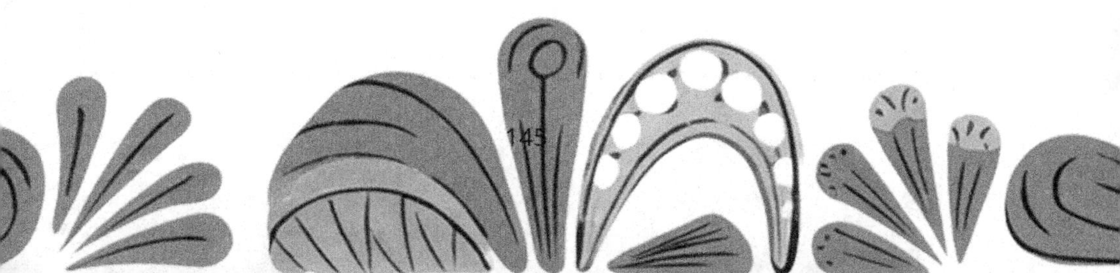

WEEK 43

Learning from Challenges

"Consider it pure joy, my brothers and sisters, whenever you face trials of many kinds, because you know that the testing of your faith produces perseverance." – James 1:2-3

REFLECTION

Challenges are never easy, but this verse shows how they can lead to growth. When you face difficulties with faith, they become opportunities to develop perseverance and deepen your trust in God. Reflecting on your challenges helps you see how God has been with you, even in the hardest moments.

WEEKLY CHALLENGE

Think about one challenge you've faced this year. Write down what you learned from it and how it strengthened your faith. Pray for continued perseverance and growth through future challenges.

Share your thoughts:

JOURNAL QUESTIONS

What's one challenge you faced this year, and how did God help you through it?

What lessons did you learn from that challenge that you can apply to the future?

How has overcoming struggles strengthened your faith and trust in God?

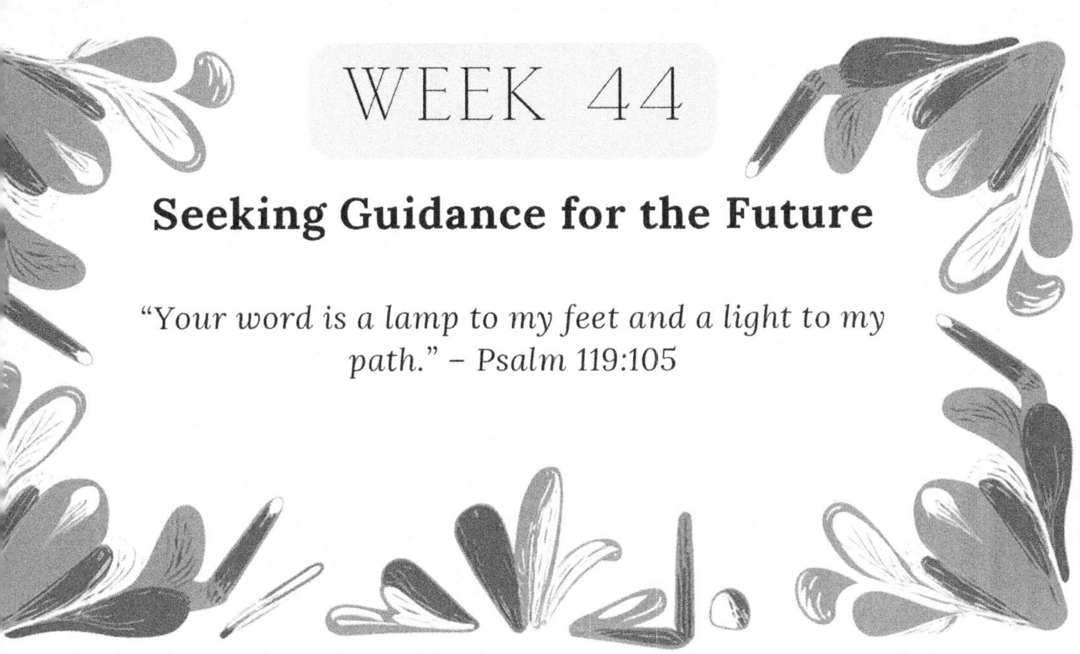

WEEK 44

Seeking Guidance for the Future

"Your word is a lamp to my feet and a light to my path." – Psalm 119:105

REFLECTION

As you look to the future, it's important to seek God's guidance. This verse reminds you that His Word is your ultimate source of direction. By staying connected to God through prayer and Scripture, you can navigate life's uncertainties with confidence, knowing He is lighting your path.

WEEKLY CHALLENGE

Pray each day this week for God's guidance in a specific area of your future. Write down any insights or encouragement you receive and reflect on how God's Word can guide your next steps.

Share your thoughts:

PRAYER TIPS

1. Pray daily for wisdom and guidance as you plan for the next chapter of your life.

2. Reflect on Proverbs 3:5-6 ("Trust in the Lord with all your heart...") and ask God to direct your steps.

3. Seek advice from a trusted mentor or family member when making big decisions.

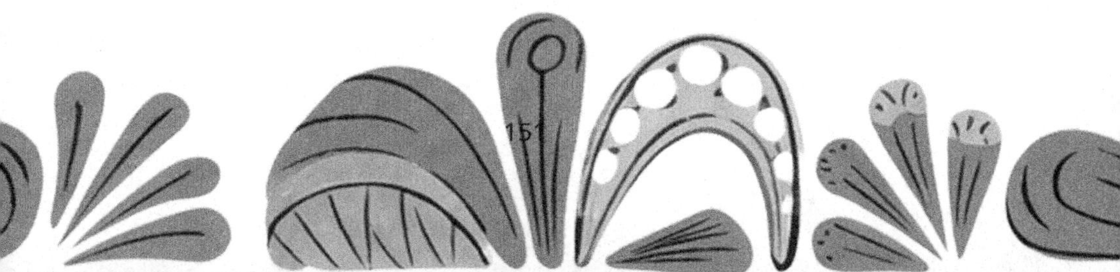

CHAPTER 12

BECOMING A LEADER IN FAITH

Leadership isn't about being the loudest or the most popular—it's about setting an example that points others to God. This chapter will teach you how to lead by example, encourage others in their faith, influence your community positively, and live with integrity and humility. Whether you realize it or not, people are watching how you live your life. By becoming a leader in faith, you can inspire others to grow closer to God.

Leading by Example

"Set an example for the believers in speech, in conduct, in love, in faith, and in purity." – 1 Timothy 4:12

REFLECTION

Leadership isn't about being in charge—it's about being an example. This verse encourages you to live in a way that inspires others, even if you're young. When your words and actions reflect your faith, you show others what it means to follow Christ. True leadership starts with integrity, kindness, and a heart devoted to God.

WEEKLY CHALLENGE

Identify one way you can lead by example this week, whether at school, in your family, or among your friends. Write down how living out your faith influences others.

Share your thoughts:

JOURNAL QUESTIONS

How can your words and actions reflect your faith to others?

Who looks up to you, and how can you be a positive role model in their life?

What's one area of your life where you want to set a better example for others?

WEEK 46

Encouraging Others in Their Faith

"Therefore encourage one another and build each other up, just as in fact you are doing." – 1 Thessalonians 5:11

REFLECTION

Everyone needs encouragement, especially in their faith journey. This verse reminds you to lift others up with your words and actions. Encouragement can be as simple as a kind word or a prayer for someone who's struggling. When you encourage others, you help them grow stronger in their relationship with God.

WEEKLY CHALLENGE

Encourage one person each day this week—through a kind message, prayer, or words of support. Reflect on how these actions strengthen your relationships and build others up.

Share your thoughts:

PRAYER TIPS

1 Send a note or text to encourage a friend in their walk with God.

2 Pray for someone who's struggling in their faith and let them know you're praying for them.

3 Be open about your own faith journey—it can inspire others to grow closer to God.

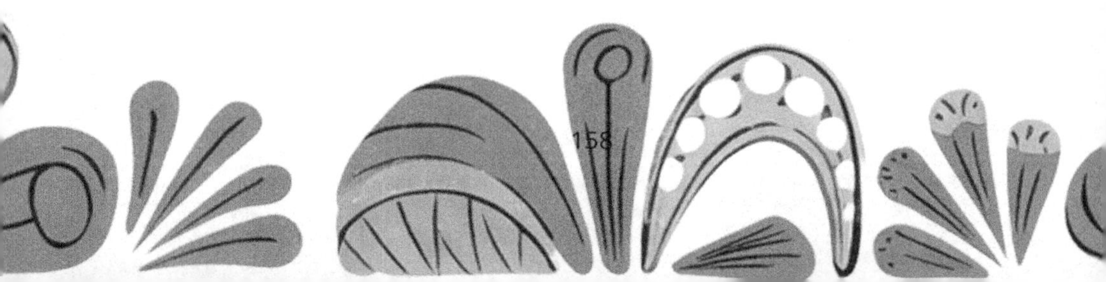

WEEK 47

Being a Positive Influence in Your Community

"Let your light shine before others, that they may see your good deeds and glorify your Father in heaven." – *Matthew 5:16*

REFLECTION

Your actions have the power to inspire and impact those around you. This verse reminds you that when you live with integrity and kindness, others will see God's love through you. Being a positive influence isn't about drawing attention to yourself—it's about pointing others to God through your example.

WEEKLY CHALLENGE

Look for one way to positively impact your community this week, whether it's helping a neighbor, volunteering, or showing kindness to someone in need. Write about how this experience reflects God's love.

Share your thoughts:

JOURNAL QUESTIONS

What's one way you can positively impact your school, neighborhood, or church this week?

____

____

____

How can showing kindness and respect point others to God?

____

____

____

What gifts or talents can you use to make a difference in your community?

____

____

____

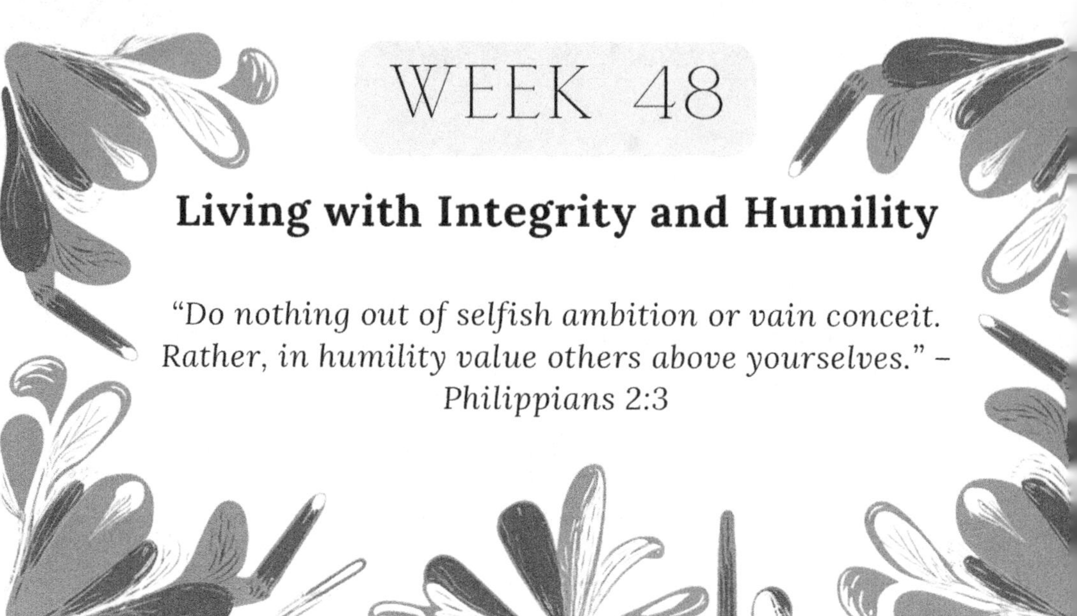

WEEK 48

Living with Integrity and Humility

"Do nothing out of selfish ambition or vain conceit. Rather, in humility value others above yourselves." – *Philippians 2:3*

REFLECTION

Integrity and humility are key traits of a strong leader. This verse challenges you to put others first, avoiding pride or selfishness. True humility comes from understanding your worth in God and serving others out of love, not for recognition. When you lead with humility, you reflect Christ's character and inspire others to do the same.

WEEKLY CHALLENGE

Practice humility this week by putting someone else's needs before your own. Reflect on how this strengthens your relationships and helps you grow in your faith.

Share your thoughts:

PRAYER TIPS

1 Be honest, even when it's hard—it builds trust and reflects God's character.

2 Practice putting others' needs before your own as an act of humility.

3 Pray for God to help you stay humble and grounded in every situation.

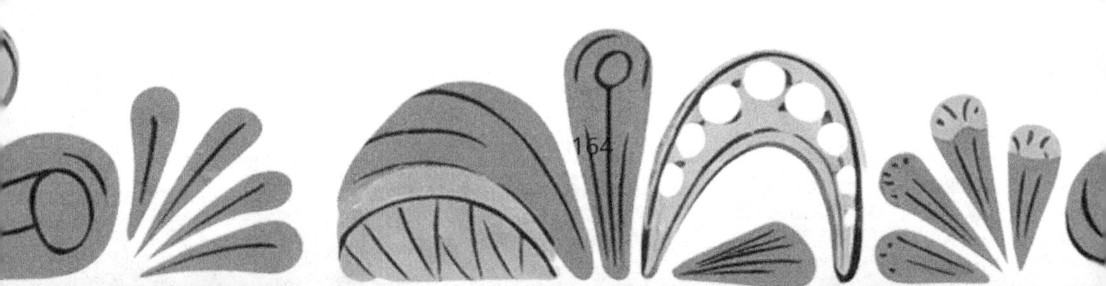

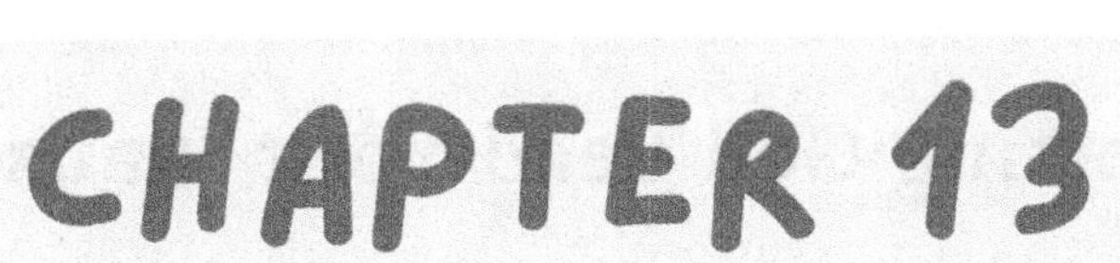

CHAPTER 13

PREPARING FOR THE NEXT CHAPTER

Your faith journey doesn't end here—it's a lifelong adventure with God. This chapter will help you prepare for what's ahead by letting God lead your plans, committing to a life of worship, trusting His future for you, and stepping boldly into a new chapter of faith. As you move forward, remember that God has big plans for your life, and He'll walk with you every step of the way.

WEEK 49

Letting God Lead Your Plans

"Many are the plans in a person's heart, but it is the Lord's purpose that prevails." – Proverbs 19:21

REFLECTION

It's natural to make plans for your future, but this verse reminds you that God's purpose is always greater. When you let God lead, you align your life with His perfect plan. Trusting Him with your future allows you to move forward with confidence, knowing He is in control.

WEEKLY CHALLENGE

Write down one goal or dream for your future. Pray daily, asking God to guide you and align your plans with His purpose. Reflect on how trusting Him brings peace about the future.

Share your thoughts:

JOURNAL QUESTIONS

What's one goal or dream you want to commit to God?

How does trusting God with your future bring you peace?

How can you remind yourself to seek God's guidance in your plans?

WEEK 50

Committing to a Life of Worship

"Therefore, I urge you, brothers and sisters, in view of God's mercy, to offer your bodies as a living sacrifice, holy and pleasing to God—this is your true and proper worship." – Romans 12:1

REFLECTION

Worship isn't just about singing songs —it's about living a life that honors God. This verse encourages you to offer every part of yourself to Him as an act of worship. When you commit to living for God, your choices, actions, and attitude reflect His glory.

WEEKLY CHALLENGE

Spend time each day this week reflecting on how you can honor God in your daily life. Write down one area where you can grow in worshiping God through your actions.

Share your thoughts:

PRAYER TIPS

1. Worship isn't just singing—honor God with your actions, words, and attitude.

2. Dedicate a specific time each week to worship through prayer, music, or reading Scripture.

3. Reflect on Romans 12:1 and ask God to help you live as a "living sacrifice."

WEEK 51

Trusting God's Plan for the Future

"The Lord will guide you always; He will satisfy your needs in a sun-scorched land and will strengthen your frame." – Isaiah 58:11

REFLECTION

As you approach the end of this year-long journey, this verse reminds you to continue trusting God's guidance. He promises to provide for your needs and strengthen you for what lies ahead. No matter what the future holds, you can walk forward with faith, knowing God is with you.

WEEKLY CHALLENGE

Reflect on how God has guided you this year. Write down your hopes for the future and commit them to God in prayer.

Share your thoughts:

JOURNAL QUESTIONS

How has trusting God's plan brought you through challenges in the past?

What's one area of your life where you still need to trust Him more?

How can you step into the future with confidence, knowing God is in control?

WEEK 52

Stepping Boldly Into a New Year of Faith

"Forget the former things; do not dwell on the past. See, I am doing a new thing!" – Isaiah 43:18-19

REFLECTION

The end of one year is the beginning of another, and this verse reminds you to leave the past behind and embrace the new things God is doing in your life. As you step boldly into the future, trust that God has incredible plans for you. Let your faith be the foundation for everything you do in the coming year.

WEEKLY CHALLENGE

Write a prayer of gratitude for the past year and a prayer of hope for the new one. Set one spiritual goal for the next year and commit to pursuing it with God's help.

Share your thoughts:

PRAYER TIPS

1 Write down one spiritual goal for the year ahead and pray for God to guide you.

2 Leave past mistakes behind—focus on the new things God is doing in your life (Isaiah 43:18-19).

3 Celebrate the start of a new chapter by thanking God for His faithfulness this year.

FINAL REFLECTIONS

Reflecting on Your Year in Prayer

You did it.

You made it through an entire year of prayer, reflection, and growth. Take a moment to think about everything you've learned and experienced over the past year. Maybe you had days when prayer came easily, and other days when it felt harder to focus. That's okay—what matters is that you kept showing up, even when it wasn't perfect.

Look back at the pages you've filled. Think about how God has been working in your life. Have you felt stronger during tough times? More confident in who you are? Closer to Him?

Every prayer you've written, every reflection you've made, is part of a bigger story—your story with God.

Ask yourself:

- How has prayer helped me in moments of stress, doubt, or fear?
- What's one thing I've learned about God this year?
- How am I different now compared to when I started this journal?

Write down your thoughts. This is a moment to celebrate how far you've come and thank God for walking with you through it all.

Spiritual Goals for the Year Ahead

Now it's time to look forward. Your faith journey doesn't stop here—in fact, this is just the beginning. Setting goals can help you stay connected to God and grow stronger in your faith.

Here are some ideas for spiritual goals that might fit where you're at:

- Start Every Morning with Prayer: Even if it's just a couple of minutes, make talking to God part of your daily routine.
- Learn More About the Bible: Pick a book of the Bible to study or find a plan to guide your reading.
- Step Up as a Leader: Look for ways to encourage your friends, help out at church, or be a role model in your family.
- Handle Challenges with Faith: Commit to trusting God when life throws curveballs.

Write down two or three goals that feel important to you. Maybe it's something small, like being more grateful, or something big, like sharing your faith with others. Pray about these goals and ask God to guide you as you work toward them.

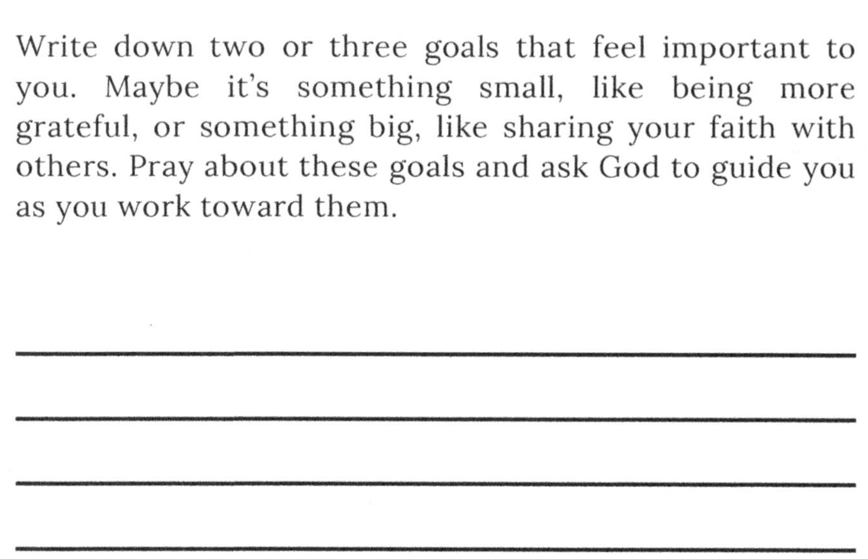

Keys to Continuing Your Faith Journey

You've built an amazing foundation for your faith this year, and now it's time to keep building on it. Here are some keys to staying strong in your relationship with God as you move forward:

1. Keep Prayer Simple and Real. You don't need fancy words or perfect timing—just talk to God. Share your struggles, your wins, and even your random thoughts. He's listening.

2. Stay Grounded in Scripture. The Bible is like your playbook for life. Read it regularly to find wisdom, direction, and encouragement.

3. Surround Yourself with Good People. Friends who share your values will help you grow stronger in your faith. Find people who inspire you and hold you accountable.

4. Be Ready to Bounce Back. Nobody's perfect, and you're going to mess up sometimes. The important thing is to get back on track. God's grace is always there for you.

5. Challenge Yourself to Grow. Keep pushing yourself to learn and try new things in your faith. Maybe it's leading a prayer group, volunteering, or talking about God with a friend who's struggling.

You're stepping into the next chapter of your life with God by your side. He's got big plans for you—plans to help you grow, succeed, and make a difference. Trust Him, lean on Him, and keep showing up.

A Final Prayer

"God, thank You for walking with me through this journey. Thank You for helping me grow, even when things were tough. As I move forward, help me stay strong in my faith, trust Your plans, and live in a way that honors You. Use my life for Your glory and help me become the young man You created me to be. Amen."

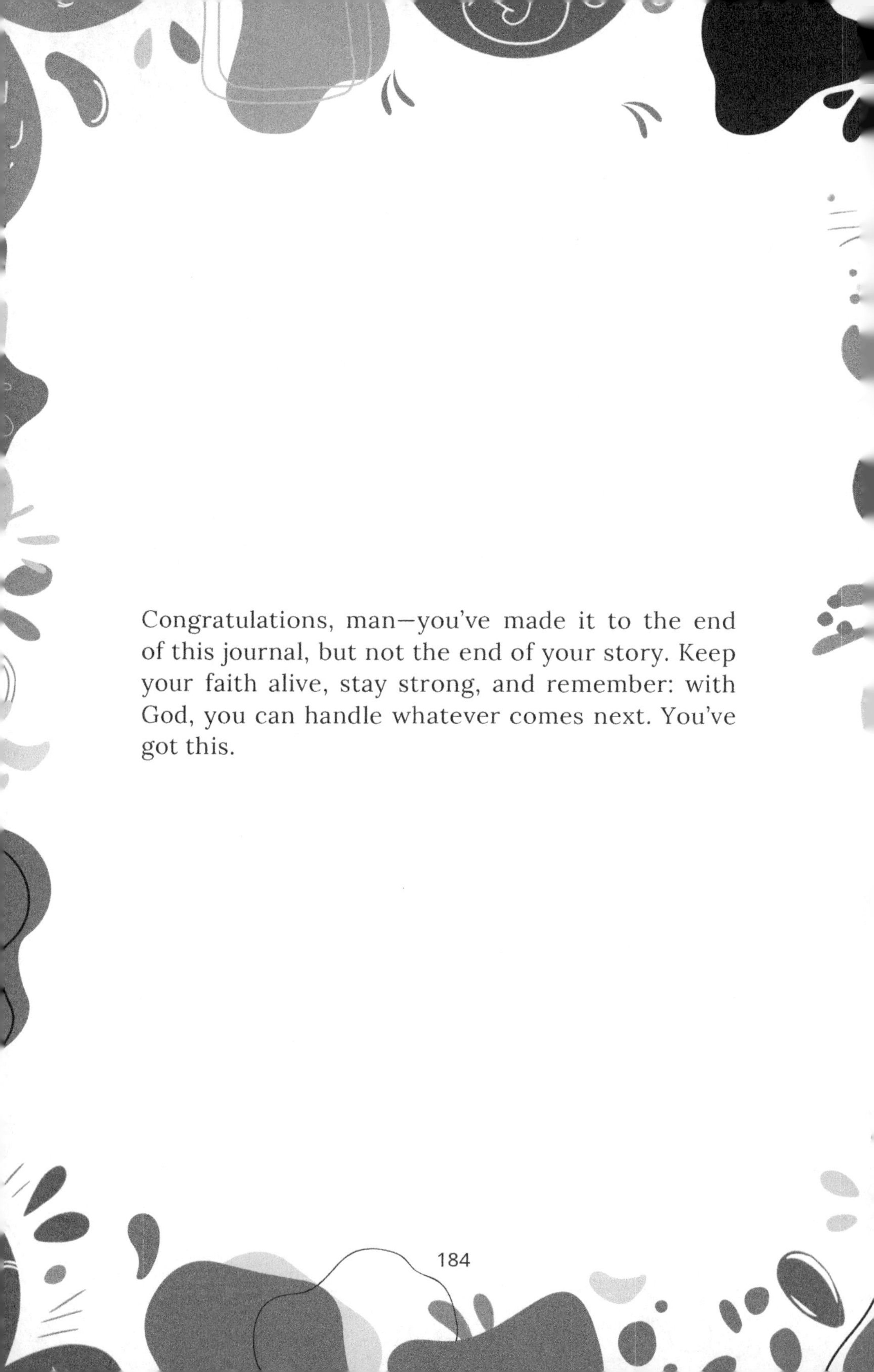

Congratulations, man—you've made it to the end of this journal, but not the end of your story. Keep your faith alive, stay strong, and remember: with God, you can handle whatever comes next. You've got this.

Made in United States
Orlando, FL
01 May 2025

60808673R00105